EMMA GOLDMAN

EMMA GOLDMAN

DAVID WALDSTREICHER

CHELSEA HOUSE PUBLISHERS

NEW YORK · PHILADELPHIA

Chelsea House Publishers
EDITOR-IN-CHIEF Nancy Toff
EXECUTIVE EDITOR Remmel T. Nunn
MANAGING EDITOR Karyn Gullen Browne
COPY CHIEF Juliann Barbato
PICTURE EDITOR Adrian G. Allen
ART DIRECTOR Maria Epes
MANUFACTURING MANAGER Gerald Levine

American Women of Achievement
SENIOR EDITOR Richard Rennert

Staff for EMMA GOLDMAN
TEXT EDITOR Constance Jones
COPY EDITOR Lisa Fenev
EDITORIAL ASSISTANTS Judith Weinstein and Nicole Claro
PICTURE RESEARCHER Andrea Reithmayr
ASSISTANT ART DIRECTOR Loraine Machlin
DESIGNER Debora Smith
LAYOUT Design Oasis
PRODUCTION MANAGER Joseph Romano
PRODUCTION COORDINATOR Marie Claire Cebrián
COVER ART Robert Caputo

First Printing

1 3 5 7 9 8 6 4 2

Library of Congress Cataloging-in-Publication Data

Waldstreicher, David.
   Emma Goldman/David Waldstreicher
     p. cm.—(American women of achievement)
   Includes bibliographical references.
   Summary: A biography of the political activist who was
imprisoned and deported for advocating such causes as anarchism, birth control, women's rights, and for opposing the
draft during World War I.
   ISBN 1-55546-655-9
      0-7910-0435-X (pbk.)
   1. Goldman, Emma, 1869–1940—Juvenile literature.
2. Anarchists—United States—Biography—Juvenile
literature. 3. Political activists—United States—Biography—
Juvenile literature. [1. Goldman, Emma, 1869–1940.
2. Anarchists. 3. Political activists.] I. Title. II. Series.
HX843.7.G65W35 1990   89-36624
[92]—dc20   CIP
                                    AC

CONTENTS

AMERICAN WOMEN OF ACHIEVEMENT

Abigail Adams
women's rights advocate

Jane Addams
social worker

Louisa May Alcott
author

Marian Anderson
singer

Susan B. Anthony
woman suffragist

Ethel Barrymore
actress

Clara Barton
*founder of the American
Red Cross*

Elizabeth Blackwell
physician

Nellie Bly
journalist

Margaret Bourke-White
photographer

Pearl Buck
author

Rachel Carson
biologist and author

Mary Cassatt
artist

Agnes de Mille
choreographer

Emily Dickinson
poet

Isadora Duncan
dancer

Amelia Earhart
aviator

Mary Baker Eddy
*founder of the Christian
Science church*

Betty Friedan
feminist

Althea Gibson
tennis champion

Emma Goldman
political activist

Helen Hayes
actress

Lillian Hellman
playwright

Katharine Hepburn
actress

Karen Horney
psychoanalyst

Anne Hutchinson
religious leader

Mahalia Jackson
gospel singer

Helen Keller
humanitarian

Jeane Kirkpatrick
diplomat

Emma Lazarus
poet

Clare Boothe Luce
author and diplomat

Barbara McClintock
biologist

Margaret Mead
anthropologist

Edna St. Vincent Millay
poet

Julia Morgan
architect

Grandma Moses
painter

Louise Nevelson
sculptor

Sandra Day O'Connor
Supreme Court justice

Georgia O'Keeffe
painter

Eleanor Roosevelt
diplomat and humanitarian

Wilma Rudolph
champion athlete

Florence Sabin
medical researcher

Beverly Sills
opera singer

Gertrude Stein
author

Gloria Steinem
feminist

Harriet Beecher Stowe
author and abolitionist

Mae West
entertainer

Edith Wharton
author

Phillis Wheatley
poet

Babe Didrikson Zaharias
champion athlete

CHELSEA HOUSE PUBLISHERS

"REMEMBER THE LADIES"

M A T I N A   S .   H O R N E R

Remember the Ladies." That is what Abigail Adams wrote to her husband, John, then a delegate to the Continental Congress, as the Founding Fathers met in Philadelphia to form a new nation in March of 1776. "Be more generous and favorable to them than your ancestors. Do not put such unlimited power in the hands of the Husbands. If particular care and attention is not paid to the Ladies," Abigail Adams warned, "we are determined to foment a Rebellion, and will not hold ourselves bound by any Laws in which we have no voice, or Representation."

The words of Abigail Adams, one of the earliest American advocates of women's rights, were prophetic. Because when we have not "remembered the ladies," they have, by their words and deeds, reminded us so forcefully of the omission that we cannot fail to remember them. For the history of American women is as interesting and varied as the history of our nation as a whole. American women have played an integral part in founding, settling, and building our country. Some we remember as remarkable women who—against great odds—achieved distinction in the public arena: Anne Hutchinson, who in the 17th century became a charismatic religious leader; Phillis Wheatley, an 18th-century black slave who became a poet; Susan B. Anthony, whose name is synonymous with the 19th-century women's rights movement and who led the struggle to enfranchise women; and, in our own century, Amelia Earhart, the first woman to cross the Atlantic Ocean by air.

These extraordinary women certainly merit our admiration, but other women, "common women," many of them all but forgotten, should also be recognized for their contributions to American thought and culture. Women have been community builders; they have founded schools and formed voluntary associations to help those in need; they have assumed the major responsibility for rearing children, passing on from one generation to the next the values that keep a culture alive. These and innumerable other contributions, once ignored, are now being recognized by scholars, students, and the public. It is exciting and gratifying to realize that a part of our history that was hardly acknowledged a few generations ago is now being studied and brought to light.

In recent decades, the field of women's history has grown from obscurity to a politically controversial splinter movement to academic respectability, in many cases mainstreamed into such traditional disciplines as history, economics, and psychology. Scholars of women, both female and male, have organized research centers at such prestigious institutions as Wellesley College, Stanford University, and the University of California. Other notable centers for women's studies are the Center for the American Woman and Politics at the Eagleton Institute of Politics at Rutgers University; the Henry A. Murray Research Center for the Study of Lives, at Radcliffe College; and the Women's Research and Education Institute, the research arm of the Congressional Caucus on Women's Issues. Other scholars and public figures have established archives and libraries, such as the Schlesinger Library on the History of Women in America, at Radcliffe College, and the Sophia Smith Collection, at Smith College, to collect and preserve the written and tangible legacies of women.

From the initial donation of the Women's Rights Collection in 1943, the Schlesinger Library grew to encompass vast collections documenting the manifold accomplishments of American women. Simultaneously, the women's movement in general and the academic discipline of women's studies in particular also began with a narrow definition and gradually expanded their mandate. Early causes such as woman suffrage and social reform, abolition and organized labor were joined by newer concerns such as the history of women in business and the professions and in politics and government; the study of the family; and social issues such as health policy and education.

Women, as historian Arthur M. Schlesinger, jr., once pointed out, "have constituted the most spectacular casualty of traditional history.

They have made up at least half the human race, but you could never tell that by looking at the books historians write." The new breed of historians is remedying that omission. They have written books about immigrant women and about working-class women who struggled for survival in cities and about black women who met the challenges of life in rural areas. They are telling the stories of women who, despite the barriers of tradition and economics, became lawyers and doctors and public figures.

The women's studies movement has also led scholars to question traditional interpretations of their respective disciplines. For example, the study of war has traditionally been an exercise in military and political analysis, an examination of strategies planned and executed by men. But scholars of women's history have pointed out that wars have also been periods of tremendous change and even opportunity for women, because the very absence of men on the home front enabled them to expand their educational, economic, and professional activities and to assume leadership in their homes.

The early scholars of women's history showed a unique brand of courage in choosing to investigate new subjects and take new approaches to old ones. Often, like their subjects, they endured criticism and even ostracism by their academic colleagues. But their efforts have unquestionably been worthwhile, because with the publication of each new study and book another piece of the historical patchwork is sewn into place, revealing an increasingly comprehensive picture of the role of women in our rich and varied history.

Such books on groups of women are essential, but books that focus on the lives of individuals are equally indispensable. Biographies can be inspirational, offering their readers the example of people with vision who have looked outside themselves for their goals and have often struggled against great obstacles to achieve them. Marian Anderson, for instance, had to overcome racial bigotry in order to perfect her art and perform as a concert singer. Isadora Duncan defied the rules of classical dance to find true artistic freedom. Jane Addams had to break down society's notions of the proper role for women in order to create new social institutions, notably the settlement house. All of these women had to come to terms both with themselves and with the world in which they lived. Only then could they move ahead as pioneers in their chosen callings.

Biography can inspire not only by adulation but also by realism. It helps us to see not only the qualities in others that we hope to emulate but also, perhaps, the weaknesses that made them "human." By helping us identify with the subject on a more personal level they help us to feel that we, too, can achieve such goals. We read about Eleanor Roosevelt, for example, who occupied a unique and seemingly enviable position as the wife of the president. Yet we can sympathize with her inner dilemma: an inherently shy woman who had to force herself to live a most public life in order to use her position to benefit others. We may not be able to imagine ourselves having the immense poetic talent of Emily Dickinson, but from her story we can understand the challenges faced by a creative woman who was expected to fulfill many family responsibilities. And though few of us will ever reach the level of athletic accomplishment displayed by Wilma Rudolph or Babe Zaharias, we can still appreciate their spirit, their overwhelming will to excel.

A biography is a multifaceted lens. It is first of all a magnification, the intimate examination of one particular life. But at the same time, it is a wide-angle lens, informing us about the world in which the subject lived. We come away from reading about one life knowing more about the social, political, and economic fabric of the time. It is for this reason, perhaps, that the great New England essayist Ralph Waldo Emerson wrote, in 1841, "There is properly no history: only biography." And it is also why biography, and particularly women's biography, will continue to fascinate writers and readers alike.

EMMA GOLDMAN

During the summer of 1893, when an economic depression gripped the United States, Emma Goldman rose to fame as a champion of the oppressed.

ONE

Ten Months for Talking

As Americans sweated through the summer of 1893 their conversation shuttled between the heat and the hard times. Neither seemed likely to let up soon. Bankers, shopkeepers, laborers, and homemakers gathered on street corners to comment on the brutal weather and discuss remedies for the most devastating economic depression the country had yet seen.

Some had more leisure for talk than others. Businesses had been failing all year, throwing thousands out of work. Unemployment continued to mount as July wore into August; tempers rose accordingly. Across the country, protests broke out. A committee of idle St. Louis rail workers occupied the city's train station and urged arriving job seekers to travel on to Washington, D.C., to make their grievances known. Laid-off farmhands in Fresno, Califor-

nia, threatened the underpaid Chinese immigrants who had replaced them. Destitute Milwaukee laborers marched to the mayor's house, demanding work and bread.

By the 1890s the enormous supply of cheap labor provided by successive waves of immigrants from abroad had made the United States a leader in the world's Industrial Revolution. American entrepreneurs had built great manufacturing empires by exploiting the impoverished immigrant work force. The owners and managers of these empires, faced with intense competition, strove to maximize the efficiency of their operations. In order to curb the costs of production, they kept workers' wages low and their hours long, and they enforced rigid workplace discipline. The factory workplace became increasingly intolerable to masses of

The Industrial Revolution of the late 19th century created a new class of urban laborers who toiled long hours in noisy, crowded, and unsafe factories such as this one.

laborers, especially after the stock market crash of June 1893. Forced to accept reduced pay and regular layoffs, wage earners bore the brunt of the losses sustained by their employers. Every citizen of the industrial city learned that the bosses made the rules.

In New York City that year, Manhattan's Lower East Side—home to the latest wave of Jewish immigrants from Eastern Europe—was the hub of discontent. Newly organized labor unions there had recently won their first important concessions from the barons of the clothing industry. But for many in the city's poorest neighborhood, the victories of the embattled unions brought too little help too late. Growing numbers of radical political activists decried the entire modern system of industrial wage labor, in which the wealthy took an ever-greater portion of the profits.

Those who espoused socialism urged workers to claim their fair share by taking over businesses and factories—capital—and even the government—the state—in the name of the common good. Others went further, insisting that a workers' revolution should aim to topple the existing order completely. There would be no true freedom or equality, these anarchists declared, until capital and its patron, the state, were eliminated. That summer in New York the anarchists, advocates of a society without government, found a new champion in a 24-year-old dressmaker named Emma Goldman.

In the midst of the depression, the city's organized labor groups made an appeal for direct aid from the state legislature. The government's refusal to grant relief sparked a number of political meetings, and Goldman attended many of them. The young immigrant woman, a five-year veteran of the anarchist movement, frequently made her way to the platform and implored audiences to forgo words for revolutionary action. Stirring up the public with such talk, anarchists replaced the Chicago World's Fair as front-page news. Headlines told of "Jews Incited to Disorder" and criticized Goldman, "the high priestess of anarchy," for fanning the flames of unrest.

Goldman enjoyed the sudden notoriety, yet she believed the real credit for the movement's momentum belonged to the people. "You are becoming brave and know your rights," she told one crowd. As she organized women for a garment workers' union, collected and distributed food for the homeless, and addressed larger and larger groups that summer, Goldman sensed the growing outrage of the working class. So did the authorities. Policemen tracked her by day; at night, meetings at which she was to speak were often not permitted to proceed. But as a week of protests climaxed at a mass rally on the evening of August 21st, Goldman knew it was no time to lie low.

Thousands packed Union Square for the demonstration that clear night. The "Joan of Arc of the social revolution," as one reporter later dubbed her, arrived at the head of a legion of female workers, waving a large red flag. Eventually

Many of the immigrant laborers who worked in New York City's factories lived on the Lower East Side, which was also the center of the city's radical movement.

she took her place on the platform; she would speak last. A plainclothes detective stood ready with paper and pen. When the meeting got under way, successive speakers urged the audience to action against politicians and business leaders. The powerful were condemned for ignoring economic injustice and for blaming immigrant workers for their own poverty and the spread of radical, "foreign" ideas such as socialism and anarchism.

By the time Goldman's turn to speak came, her own enthusiasm matched that of the crowd. Slightly plump and just over five feet tall, with light brown hair and blue eyes, she hardly seemed imposing as she stood to address the throng. But the passionate conviction with which she spoke soon gripped her listeners. She held forth first in English and then in Yiddish-accented German, urging native and immigrant working people to join against their common enemies, capital and the state:

You thought this was a free country.
You thought you would be free here

because there is no czar and no king, [but] the capitalist takes your muscle, profits by your labor, and throws you out into the street, sick, suffering, and hungry. . . .

The government does nothing for you. . . . You are used by the politicians for their purposes, whether they are Republican or Democrat. . . . [They] drink champagne and treat you only as their tools.

Pandemonium broke out when she concluded: "Demonstrate before the palaces of the rich; demand work. If they do not give you work, demand bread. If they deny you both, take bread. It is your sacred right!"

Hundreds followed "Red Emma" down Broadway after the rally. To evade the police who tailed her, she boarded a streetcar uptown and after a few stops switched to a downtown car, proceeding home alone. The next day Goldman slipped out of New York and traveled to Philadelphia, where it seemed the authorities were less likely to find her. But a few days later the police arrested her as she entered a hall to give a speech. Whisked back to New York, Goldman received a solemn offer from the chief of police: He would grant her full immunity from prosecution if she would keep him informed of the activities of the East Side radicals. Goldman scorned the invitation and was charged with three counts of inciting to riot.

In a matter of weeks Emma Goldman had become, as she put it, "an important personage." Supporters formed an Emma Goldman Defense Fund and raised money for her bail; a former

Newspaper artists frequently sketched Goldman, a leading figure in the workers' uprisings of 1893. Some reporters dubbed her "the high priestess of anarchy."

mayor of New York volunteered to serve as her attorney. Renowned journalist Nellie Bly of the *New York World* visited the anarchist in her cell for a lengthy interview. Bly expected to meet a fanatic babbling about bombs, but instead she found "a little bit of a girl," neatly dressed. Calm and gracious, Goldman grew earnest when she described her calling. "I am an anarchist and give my life to the cause," she told Bly, "for only through it can be ended all suffering and want and unhappiness."

After Goldman's arrest, Nellie Bly (above), a reporter for the New York World, *interviewed the anarchist and wrote an unusually flattering newspaper article about her.*

The *World* published Bly's sympathetic article on Goldman, but the other papers were not so kind. The *New York Times*, for instance, reported that at her arraignment Goldman "as-sumed an air of martyrdom ridiculous to all except the great army of the unwashed." Knowing full well that fame, in her case, did not mean popularity, Goldman expected to receive the maximum penalty for her actions. Nonetheless, she hoped to use her trial to publicize anarchist ideas.

In the courtroom Goldman took every opportunity to express her belief in free speech and her opposition to all forms of government. The prosecution considered her beliefs, especially her atheism, incriminating. They construed her Union Square cry to "take bread" as an exhortation to riot. The defense contended that Goldman had preached peaceful demonstration, not outright destruction, and that her speech had caused no actual riot. At the close of the 6-day trial the jury of 12 middle-class men deliberated for 2 hours and returned a verdict of guilty. Sentencing Goldman to one year in the penitentiary on Blackwell's Island (now Roosevelt Island) in New York's East River, the judge gave his own evaluation of the defendant and her ideas: "You have told us that you do not believe in our institutions. Such a person cannot be tolerated in this community. I look upon you as a dangerous woman in your doctrines."

Prison emboldened Goldman, increasing her disdain for the claims of authority. As overseer of the sewing shop, she earned the admiration of her fellow inmates by refusing to serve, as she put it, as a "slave driver." While recovering from a bout of rheumatism in the prison infirmary, she impressed the house doctor with her kindness to other patients. He had her assigned as a practical nurse, and she began to learn a skill that would be her bread and butter for many years. In her spare time, Goldman relieved the tedium and loneliness of confinement by trading favors with the other women and sharing the food sent her by admirers. She read books sent by friends, thus broadening her education and improving her English.

Instead of withering in prison, Goldman came to regard it as "a school of experience." She later wrote that she "learned to see life through my own eyes" in prison, and that her time there "helped me to discover . . . the strength to live my life and fight for my ideals." After 10 wearying yet valuable months on Blackwell's Island, Goldman gained parole on August 17, 1894. Landing at the dock in Manhattan, she boarded a streetcar and then switched to another, this time to avoid reporters rather than police.

Twenty-eight hundred people filled a downtown theater that evening to welcome Goldman home. In seven languages speakers praised the anarchist's courage, fortitude, and dedication to the cause. Finally, amid shouts and applause, the guest of honor rose and made her own remarks. "I have come back to you after having served 10 months in prison for talking," she said. "But it was not Emma Goldman who was prosecuted. It was the thoughts of

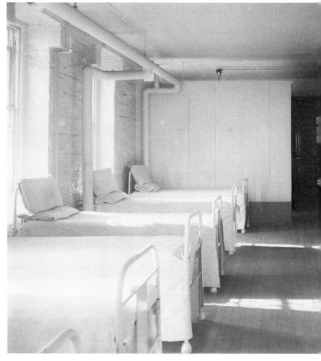

Goldman learned a new profession, nursing, while confined to the prison on Blackwell's Island. She spent many hours caring for ailing inmates in the infirmary.

Emma Goldman, the principles of Anarchy. . . . It was the right of free speech that was prosecuted in the Court of General Sessions, and not little Emma Goldman."

By refusing to be silenced, Emma Goldman became a hero to all who champion an unpopular ideal. Her refusal to accept the world as she found it would win for her a reputation as the most dangerous woman in America.

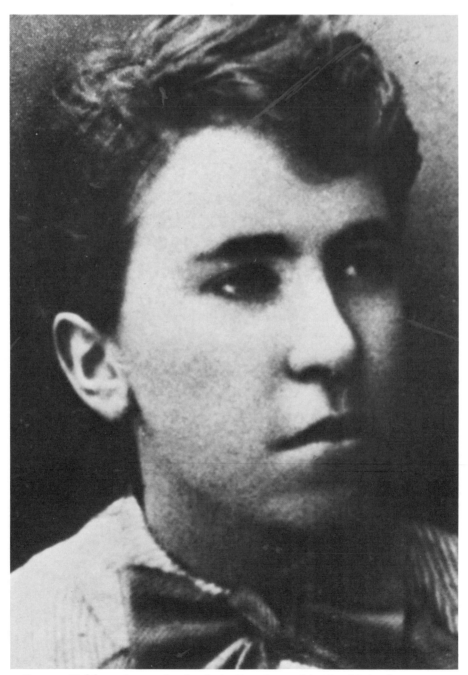

Emma Goldman's youth—both in Russia and in the United States—was marked by economic hardship and by abuse at the hands of relatives, teachers, and employers.

T W O

The Causes of a Rebel

W hat I have seen meted out to others by authority and repression," Emma Goldman once wrote, ". . . transcends anything I myself may have endured." Goldman interpreted anarchism as the effort to liberate all people from oppressive social conventions. Her dedication to the cause had as much to do with her own origins as with the economic and political injustices she witnessed during her life. Early experience shaped her dream of freedom and laid the foundation for her lifelong crusade against restrictive institutions and customs.

Political and social uncertainty plagued the Lithuanian province of Kovno (now Kaunas) where Emma Goldman was born on June 27, 1869. Most of Russia's Jews were forced to live on that westernmost edge of the empire—formerly part of Poland, it was known as the Pale of Settlement—and were forcibly kept on the very margins of Russian society. Official edicts dictated where they could live, how they could earn a living, and how many could attend school. The government sponsored anti-Semitic pogroms—vicious riots in which Jews were beaten and murdered—to keep them in a state of submission.

Most Russian Jews eked out a living in the ghetto villages of the Pale, finding some comfort in the traditions of family and faith. The Goldmans never quite fit that mold. Emma's parents came from middle-class families and had great expectations for their future. But their hopes were crushed as the restrictions placed on Jews grew ever tighter and as their marriage crumbled under the strain. Their family life was disappointing, for the Goldman mar-

Abraham Goldman, Emma's father, was an educated man whose ambitions were thwarted by czarist Russia's oppression of Jews. He often took out his frustrations on his family.

riage was the product of an arranged match—or mismatch. When she married Abraham Goldman, Taube Bienowitz still grieved for her first husband, who had died and left her with two daughters. Soon after their marriage, her new husband lost her inheritance in a failed business venture. Emma's birth one year later was not a happy occasion: Abraham blamed Taube for not producing a boy.

In 1870, Abraham Goldman landed a job as an innkeeper and caretaker of the government stagecoach in Popelan, a Lithuanian town near the Baltic Sea.

The position provided a decent income but proved highly stressful. Drunken patrons at the inn hurled ethnic slurs at their Jewish hosts; government officials accused Abraham Goldman of contributing to peasant drunkenness. The arrival of three more children during the next five years only increased tensions in the household. Taube Goldman grew cold and distant, her husband increasingly short-tempered. The mischievous Emma was beaten regularly for displeasing her father. Only Helena, the younger of Emma's two half sisters, showed the young girl any affection.

Emma turned for friendship to other village children and to the servants at the inn. Early on she saw her friends abused by those in power. Officers from the czar's army forced peasants into military service. Soldiers seduced women and abandoned them. Emma's friends at the inn were frequently fired by her parents for minor infractions. Ultimately, Abraham Goldman lost his own job when a rival for the post bribed his superior.

When she was seven years old Emma traveled alone to the Prussian city of Königsberg (now Kaliningrad in the Soviet Union) to live with her grandmother and attend a private school. The recent death of a younger brother and the illness of both her parents made this a welcome change for all. But soon after Emma's arrival her grandmother left to tend a sick relative, putting an uncle in charge of the household. Emma's uncle took her out of school, forced her to serve as his domestic slave, and pocketed the funds her father sent to pay for board and school. When Emma finally protested, her uncle kicked her down a flight of stairs. Neighbors rescued her, and her father took her home.

Emma's formal education actually began a year later, when the whole family moved to Königsberg. She entered a public school, where she witnessed further abuses of power. The religion teacher beat his students' hands with a ruler; the geography teacher sexually molested girls he kept after class. Unwilling to accept such treatment passively, Emma organized pranks against her religion teacher, even though it made her a special target of punishment. She resisted the geography teacher's advances, eventually causing his dismissal.

Only one of her instructors, a teacher of German, seemed genuinely interested in Emma's education. She introduced her student to the world of literature—specifically, to romantic novels, which they read together on many afternoons after school. The teacher saw potential in Emma and encouraged her to work hard in all her classes. Emma thrived under her teacher's attention, finding refuge in her studies. Soon, however, her education came to an end. When her parents decided to move to St. Petersburg, then the Russian capital, 13-year-old Emma had no choice but to go with them.

Abraham Goldman took a job managing a cousin's dry-goods store, and to help support the family the Goldman sisters went to work. Emma knitted shawls at home; later she took a job in

Although active in community work and important to the family's economic survival, Taube Goldman, Emma's mother, provided her children with little emotional support.

a glove factory. Although she was disappointed that she could not continue her schooling, Emma found that her new life had its rewards. St. Petersburg hummed with all kinds of cultural and social activity, and especially with political activity. Czar Alexander II had been assassinated a year earlier, in 1881. Emma met students—friends of her elder sisters—who spoke earnestly of the revolutionists who had committed the deed in the name of the op-

Socialist radicals assassinated Czar Alexander II a year before the Goldmans moved to the Russian capital, St. Petersburg. Emma found the city's revolutionary atmosphere exciting.

pressed Russian masses. She felt an immediate sympathy for the socialist rebels.

To learn more about their cause, Emma and her sister Helena read the forbidden books of radical writers. The one that most impressed Emma was a novel entitled *What Is to Be Done?* written by Nikolay Chernyshevsky in 1863. Vera, the story's protagonist, rejects custom and refuses to marry for financial security. Instead, she opens a cooperative dress shop, hoping to earn enough money to attend medical school. Vera takes part in the revolutionary movement and dreams of a world without government, church, or other structures of authority. The Goldman sisters were inspired by Vera's vision of a world in which people, unencumbered by social conventions, further the public good by seeking individual fulfillment. Emma Goldman's speeches would someday echo Vera's goals of economic justice for workers, liberation for women, and a revolution for universal personal freedom.

But first Emma would have to struggle for her own freedom. She spent more and more time away from her unhappy home, and her father became increasingly suspicious. He decided to marry off his daughter before she "disgraced" herself and the family. Set firmly against the idea, Emma constantly argued with her father, often bearing his angry blows. At 15, she incurred his wrath by insisting she would marry for love alone. Mocking her plans to study and travel, Abraham Goldman told his daughter, "Girls do not have to learn much! All a Jewish daughter needs to know is how to prepare gefilte fish, cut noodles fine, and give the man plenty of children."

A frustrating stalemate ensued. Still toiling at the glove factory, Emma looked for a way to live her own life rather than the one dictated by her father. Fortunately, a solution to the problem soon emerged. Helena Goldman decided to leave Russia for the United States, where the eldest Goldman sister, Lena, had already settled. Helena asked Emma to come with her. After weeks of argument ending with Emma's threat to drown herself, Abraham Goldman consented. The two sisters traveled to Hamburg, Germany, where they purchased steamship tickets to New York City.

For the half-million Jewish immigrants who left Eastern Europe during the late 19th century, America was imbued with all the imagery of the biblical Promised Land. But disappointment greeted the Goldman sisters when they landed in the New World on December 29, 1885. Immigration offi-

cials at New York's Castle Garden, the reception point for entering foreigners, seemed as callous and arrogant as the czar's soldiers. Sixteen-year-old Emma was surprised to find that the authorities did not seem to care about the condition or fate of the newcomers. After enduring lengthy and degrading clearance procedures, the sisters eagerly departed for Lena's home in Rochester, New York.

There the reception proved warmer. Lena Goldman Comminsky, expecting her first child, had prepared a room for her sisters in her small apartment. The

As an adult, Goldman wrote that Catherine Breshkovskaya (pictured) and other women active in Russia's radical movement "had been my inspiration ever since I had first read of their lives."

An 1882 Goldman family portrait shows Emma behind Helena, who holds Morris in her lap; Herman stands in the center, and Taube and Abraham are seated at the table.

new arrivals soon found jobs: Helena at a photography store, Emma at Garson & Mayer's clothing factory, where she sewed overcoats 6 days a week, 10½ hours each day. The weekly wage of $2.50 left Emma little to contribute to her room and board and even less to spend on occasional luxuries such as a book or a theater ticket. "These were my early lessons in American liberty," she would recall dryly. When her boss refused her a raise, Emma secured a position in a smaller factory that offered better pay and less oppressive working conditions. There, workers were allowed to chat while working and to take occasional breaks. At the sewing machine next to Emma's sat another Russian immigrant, Jacob Kershner. The handsome young man shared her interest in books and soon began to court her formally. During the summer of 1886 she agreed to his proposal of marriage.

Soon afterward, the rest of the Goldman family fled worsening conditions in St. Petersburg and made their way to Rochester. Lena Comminsky and her growing family stayed in their own tiny home while the six other Goldmans crowded into four rooms and took in a boarder—Jacob Kershner—for extra cash. Close contact revealed the limits of her fiancé's charm and intellect, but marriage promised Emma greater independence from her family. The couple wed in February 1887. Married life, however, fell short of all Goldman's expectations. Kershner, it turned out, was impotent. Driven perhaps to demonstrate his manhood in other ways, he forbade his wife to work outside the home, turned irrationally jealous, and gambled away much of his

income. Goldman, feeling frustrated and trapped, began to look elsewhere for fulfillment.

Just as Goldman's stay in St. Petersburg had coincided with a revolutionary movement, her first years in the United States were marked by waves of labor protest. America appeared to be evolving into two nations: One was made up of wage earners who toiled in the growing industrial workplace, the other of business and property owners who controlled that workplace. The laborers were generally struggling immigrants and their children, who sought to improve their lot by demanding higher pay and better working conditions. Their employers, most often the members of established American families, regarded the workers' complaints as threats to the community and nation.

In 1885, Emma and her sister Helena boarded a steamship crowded with other immigrants and traveled to the United States. They joined their sister Lena in Rochester, New York.

At an anarchist rally held in Chicago's Haymarket Square on May 7, 1886, a bomb exploded and set off a riot. Dozens were killed or wounded, and eight of the protesters were arrested.

Most laborers active in the movement for a better workplace wanted to secure the right to organize into unions and strike if necessary to secure such demands as the eight-hour working day. Employers, however, preferred to maintain a loosely defined system of individualized employer-to-employee bargaining. They claimed that one-on-one agreements provided every person with equal opportunity to advance according to his or her talents. The police and the courts entered into the dispute on the side of management, arresting and prosecuting strike leaders for "restraint of trade" and protecting strike-breakers. Governmental intervention only increased laborers' resentment of the rich and powerful.

Events ignited passions on both sides. After a violent confrontation between police and strikers at Chicago's McCormick Harvester Company on May 7, 1886, several local anarchist leaders called a mass meeting at Haymarket Square the next evening. A light rain kept the gathering small, and the rally had almost ended when police arrived and ordered the speakers to stop. Without warning, a bomb exploded in the crowd of police officers. In the ensuing uproar dozens of demonstrators and police suffered injuries, some of them fatal.

The incident made headlines across the country, especially when the press learned the identity of several of the meeting's organizers. Among them were revolutionists who called for the destruction of the state and the seizure of capital by the workers. The nation went wild with paranoia over labor activists, foreigners (many leaders of the anarchist movement were immigrants), and political radicals of all kinds. Millions of Americans saw the immigrant radicals as importers of chaos who had to be stopped. Though the authorities could find no evidence to link any of them to the bomb, eight of the Haymarket anarchists were arraigned for murder.

The Haymarket events obsessed Emma Goldman. Much as the Russian radicals had, the anarchists on trial for their revolutionary beliefs gained her passionate empathy. Goldman started attending weekly discussions at the local German socialist club. She read everything she could on radical causes and tried to make sense of the varying accounts she heard of the episode in

Chicago. Then, at a cousin's home she picked up a copy of *Die Freiheit*, a weekly anarchist newspaper published in New York by Johann Most. The paper burned with the rhetoric of revolt and inspired Goldman with a fervent belief in anarchism. When news came in November 1887 that four of the Chicago anarchists had been hanged, Goldman felt it was a tragic blow: "I wept for their fate," she later wrote. In years to come she would cite that "Black Friday" as the day she became the "spiritual child" of the Haymarket martyrs, determined to continue their work.

Filled with new energy, Goldman ignored the protests of her inattentive husband and obtained a rabbinical divorce. She left Rochester for New Haven, Connecticut, where she secured work in a corset factory. Discovering a vibrant radical circle there, she increased her knowledge of socialism and anarchism. After a few months, however, illness forced her back to Rochester, where she stayed with her newlywed sister Helena and in time returned to work.

Kershner learned of his ex-wife's return and badgered Goldman for a reconciliation. She gave in when he threatened suicide, but remarried life only renewed the old misery. Once again she planned an escape. To augment her earning power she studied dressmaking in secret, then she finally left Kershner for good. "I was immediately ostracized by the whole Jewish population of Rochester," she recalled in *Living My Life*, her autobiography.

After four of the Haymarket anarchists were hanged, Goldman determined "to dedicate myself to the memory of my martyred comrades, to make their cause my own."

"My parents forbade me their home, and again it was only Helena who stood by me."

Goldman decided to move to New York City. Saddened to leave Helena, her beloved niece Stella Comminsky, and her youngest brother, Morris, she was nonetheless finished with the world of traditional marriage and family. It was time to seek a different life.

*In 1889, filled with "a burning faith" in the anarchist cause, Goldman
divorced her husband, moved to New York City, and plunged into life
as a radical activist.*

THREE

"A Beautiful Ideal"

On a sweltering Sunday morning in August 1889, 20-year-old Emma Goldman emerged from Grand Central Station carrying a small handbag, $5.00 cash, and two vital scraps of paper. One was a claim ticket for her sewing machine, checked as baggage. The other listed the addresses of a relative, an anarchist friend, and the Brooklyn editorial offices of *Die Freiheit*.

After wandering the New York City streets for three hours, Goldman finally found her aunt's flat. The family welcomed her but could not hide their unspoken dismay at the sudden prospect of another lodger. Disappointed, Goldman sought out and found the comrade she had met in New Haven. Hillel Solotaroff's friendly countenance and enthusiastic description of the New York anarchist circle helped allay the newcomer's anxieties. He took her

over to Sachs', a Lower East Side café where Yiddish- and Russian-speaking socialists and anarchists often congregated. There Goldman met Anna and Helen Minkin, sisters who offered to rent her their spare room. She accepted the offer over dinner, then met more of Solotaroff's friends. One of the people introduced to her that evening was a broad-shouldered young man named Alexander "Sasha" Berkman.

Berkman wasted no time in inviting the newcomer to attend an evening lecture. The speaker was to be Johann Most, editor of *Die Freiheit* and author of an instruction manual for amateur bomb builders. Most was frequently lampooned in political cartoons as the quintessential rabble-rousing immigrant radical. Middle-aged, short of stature, his face disfigured by a scar, he hardly seemed the type to inspire the

Goldman met Alexander Berkman on her first day in New York City. The two idealists initiated a close political and personal relationship that would last almost 50 years.

masses. But when he spoke, he never failed to electrify his audience. That night, Most's tribute to the Haymarket martyrs and his passionate condemnation of government awed Goldman. She could barely mumble a greeting when led to the podium for an introduction to the great German orator. Thrilled by the events of the evening, she hardly slept her first night in New York.

The next day Berkman visited Goldman in her room and asked her to join him as he called on Most. On the train ride to the *Freiheit* office she learned

much about Berkman. Just 18 years of age, he too had lived in St. Petersburg and found inspiration in the deeds and writings of the czar's assassins and their sympathizers. He too had left Russia after troubles at home and school, and he too cited Haymarket as proof that tyranny flourished in the New World as well as the Old. Goldman, impressed by Berkman's fervent commitment and touched by their common experiences, felt more than an intellectual attraction to the radical cigar maker. They spent much time together in the next months and soon became lovers.

Unlike her past in Rochester, which she described as "colorless," Goldman's life in New York was busy, exciting, and fulfilling from the first. She first took a job at a corset factory, then quit to sew piecework and make dresses on her own in a rented room on the Lower East Side. At the same time, she volunteered to stuff envelopes and run errands at the *Freiheit* office. She made many friends in the radical movement and soon attracted the attention of its leaders. Johann Most, charmed by Goldman's commitment, good looks, and quick wit, gave her more and more of his attention. After listening to her dramatic account of her life story, he resolved to train her as a speaker for the cause.

"Most became my idol," Goldman wrote 40 years later. "I worshipped him." Although she gently rebuffed his romantic overtures, she felt great sympathy for the renowned yet desperately lonely man, who was constantly hounded and often jailed by his enemies. Exploring the nature of her attachment to Berkman, Goldman found room in her heart for close companionship with another. It felt right to be bound personally as well as politically to her fellows in the movement. Johann Most provided her with valuable insight into the theories and techniques of radical activists. Under his tutelage, Goldman made her initial public appearances, delivering several short speeches at meetings held to commemorate the Haymarket executions. Soon, she left on a brief tour to address German-American labor groups on the struggle for the eight-hour workday.

Oddly, Goldman's first stop was Rochester. After a joyous reunion with her sister Helena, a nervous Goldman gave her first major oration. To her surprise, it was a rousing success. "I could sway people with words!" she recalled in *Living My Life*. "Strange magic words . . . welled up from within me, from some unfamiliar depth. I wept with the joy of knowing."

But her talent as a speaker was not always enough to persuade audiences. In Buffalo, New York, Goldman gave a lengthy speech that echoed Most's ridicule of the eight-hour-day movement. Only revolutionary action and the overthrow of the capitalist system could truly improve the lot of workers, Goldman argued; labor negotiation and government legislation could not. An elderly laborer rose and objected. The revolution of which Goldman spoke surely would not come for many years, he asserted; why not fight for specific

change in the meantime? She could not answer him, for Most himself had no reasoned response to that question.

Upon returning to New York, Goldman had a bitter argument with Most that she later said taught her "the need for independent thinking." Her mentor demanded the absolute loyalty and ideological agreement of his followers, but Goldman had begun to realize she had ideas of her own. And too often, Most seemed more interested in her as a desirable woman than as a comrade with a sharp political mind. Disillu-

Johann Most, a leader of New York's radical community, took a keen interest in Goldman until she began to question some of his ideas.

sioned, Goldman gradually distanced herself from Most and his circle.

Goldman's instinctive rebellion against Most's dictatorial impulses confirmed her devotion to anarchism's guiding principle: freedom for the individual. Other revolutionary creeds, such as socialism and communism, struck her as mechanistic, bound by rigid theories of how classes of people behave under particular economic conditions. Anarchism, on the other hand, Goldman saw as a commitment to freedom as a way of life—freedom from what she believed were the harmful constraints of laws and customs. Such liberty, she felt, would allow people to grow as individuals and would spur their natural tendency to work together for the good of the many.

In this spirit of cooperation, Goldman, Berkman, Berkman's cousin Modest "Modska" Stein, and two other friends attempted to establish a communal household. They moved into a four-room apartment, resolving to share all resources and responsibilities and pledging their collective efforts to the revolution. Conflicting ideals, however, sometimes hampered their experiment in communal living. Berkman's strong insistence on strict frugality clashed with the need and desire of Goldman and Stein, an artist, for beautiful things. "I did not believe," Goldman wrote in her autobiography, "that a cause which stood for a beautiful ideal, for anarchism, for release and freedom from conventions and prejudice, should demand the denial of life and joy."

Indeed, Berkman's grave and all-consuming dedication to anarchism both attracted and repelled Goldman. She felt increasingly drawn to the gentler Stein, who shared her appreciation of beauty and her belief that anarchism amounted to nothing if it did not free the human spirit. Goldman's certainty that love too could be free deepened when she found her devotion to Sasha undiminished by her new passion for Modska. Berkman, meanwhile, had been cultivating a relationship with Anna Minkin; now he moved out to give Goldman and Stein room for themselves. Later that year, Berkman, Stein, and Goldman moved into a new apartment together.

Living with fellow anarchists and sewing all day to support her calling as an activist, Goldman was completely immersed in the cause. She would later speak of these years as a time when she had "no personal life," for she devoted all her waking hours to anarchism. During the cloakmakers' strike of 1890, one of the first successful labor protests staged by immigrant women, Goldman spent weeks campaigning among working Jewish women, beseeching them to join the garment workers' union. Her attention was then diverted by the revival of revolutionary activity in Russia, which prompted a plan to send Berkman there to publish an anarchist paper. Over the course of the next 18 months Goldman and the other commune members repeatedly switched jobs and apartments in an effort to raise enough money for this and other revolutionary ventures.

Industrialists such as Henry Clay Frick and his partner Andrew Carnegie (inset), whose New York mansion is shown here, built huge fortunes by exploiting a largely immigrant work force.

Berkman moved to New Haven to learn the printing trade, accompanied by Stein, Goldman, and the Minkin sisters. The women tried to fulfill Goldman's longtime dream of a dress-making collective, but the effort proved unprofitable, and they had to take factory jobs to supplement their income. Goldman did much of the cooking and housework for the group, yet still found time to organize lectures and anarchist "socials." Eventually, financial and personal problems forced the group to postpone its plans to send Berkman to Russia. They returned to New York, where life resumed its previous busy pattern.

A year later, at the end of 1891, Stein moved to Springfield, Massachusetts, where a photographer had offered him good wages. Goldman obtained work in the same shop and joined him, soon followed by Berkman. Encouraged by the prosperity of their employer, the trio attempted to launch their own portrait studio in nearby Worcester. When that experiment failed, they opened a business that made better use of Stein's gift for design and Goldman's culinary talents: a luncheonette and ice cream parlor. Financial success fed their hope of taking part in the creation of a new Russia—until events closer to home seized everyone's attention.

In the summer of 1892 all America was abuzz over the shocking events at the Homestead Steel mill in western Pennsylvania. Homestead chairman Henry Clay Frick had taken advantage of the union's expiring contract to cut wages for all plant workers. When con-fronted by the union, the Amalgamated Association of Iron and Steel Workers, Frick refused to compromise. Instead he announced that the company would bargain with employees on a one-to-one basis only. Frick then locked the protesting employees out of the plant, prompting the union to call a strike.

The young anarchists in Worcester mistook public sympathy for the embattled workers for the beginnings of a popular revolution. In response to the lockout, Goldman, Berkman, and Stein sold their ice cream store and boarded a train for New York, where they would prepare for agitation in Pennsylvania. Goldman later wrote that revolutionary slogans "lost their meaning" the following week when violence erupted between strikers and plant guards. Homestead management attempted to transport 300 armed guards up the Monongahela River to protect the non-union workers who had replaced the strikers in the steel mill. When strikers attempted to prevent the guards from assuming their posts, fighting broke out. Sixteen people were killed and many more wounded on both sides. The governor called in the state militia to preserve order and to protect the strike-breakers, which ensured the union's defeat.

Berkman declared the time ripe for an *attentat*, an act designed to publicize a cause and garner support for it. He envisioned this attentat as a violent blow struck in the name of the people against the symbol of oppression, Henry Clay Frick. By assassinating Frick, he hoped to dramatize the plight

In 1892, Goldman, Berkman, and their comrades were moved to action by events at the Homestead Steel mill, where striking workers clashed with guards sent to protect strikebreakers.

of the working class and incite laborers to rebellion. Berkman, Goldman, and Stein set about secretly planning the venture and raising funds for it. Goldman managed to borrow some money from her sister Helena so Berkman could purchase a pistol and a new suit. Berkman also obtained a poison capsule with which to take his own life before the authorities could execute him. With the little money left over, the trio could afford only one train ticket to Pittsburgh, so Berkman set off alone. Goldman and Stein remained in New York to explain the act to the press.

The attentat conspiracy proved an utter failure. Berkman entered Frick's office in the guise of an employment agency owner, fired his pistol twice, and stabbed Frick several times before being overcome by carpenters at work in the adjoining room. The police arrested Berkman and took the suicide capsule from his mouth before he could use it. Frick survived the attack, winning a wave of sympathy because of his wounds. Failing to fathom Berkman's purpose, the public at first thought his act to have been provoked by personal grievances or ambitions. But his political purpose and immigrant status were soon revealed, intensifying popular hostility toward both anarchists and foreigners as advocates of violence and chaos. Even fellow anarchists criticized the attentat, questioning Berkman's motives and repudiating the use of force. Summarily tried and convicted, Berkman was sentenced to serve 22 years at the Western Penitentiary in Pennsylvania.

Goldman was one of the few to stand by Berkman, defending him against critics and organizing appeals for the reduction of his sentence. Hoping to charge her with complicity in the assassination attempt, police raided her room but failed to find any evidence of her involvement. The press also attacked her as a coconspirator, and her frightened roommate turned her out. The notorious Goldman could not even rent a new place: "My name seemed to frighten the landlords," she wrote. The only lodging she could find was a room in a brothel, and even that was temporary.

Worse even than the public's ill will was Johann Most's condemnation of the attentat and its perpetrator. Most had formerly advocated the use of terrorist tactics in the name of anarchism, but now he reversed his position, leading a majority of the radical community to do the same. Infuriated by his betrayal, Goldman appeared at a Most lecture and demanded he explain his attacks on Berkman. When the speaker dismissed her as a "hysterical woman," she produced a horsewhip from under her coat, rushed the platform, and lashed her former mentor. Shocked friends finally carried her out of the hall, leaving the gathering in an uproar.

Goldman failed to find much support for her efforts to justify Berkman's deed or free him from prison. Guilt—that she remained free while her beloved languished in jail—fed what she termed her "all-embracing devotion" to Berkman. Throughout his years in prison she would write to him regularly and

A newspaper artist's depiction of Berkman's attentat *shows Frick (in beard) speaking with a colleague as Berkman lunges at him with a pistol.*

send him books, home-cooked food, and other essentials. She gradually gave up the notion that violence was an acceptable tool for the revolutionist, but she remained loyal to Berkman. Goldman would always hold that political assassinations were the inevitable rebellions of sensitive souls against social wrongs.

Meanwhile, Berkman's suffering in solitary confinement gave Goldman yet another martyr to venerate. The split in the anarchist movement over Berkman's act cost her supporters, but it also strengthened her dedication to the "beautiful ideal." She toured the major cities of the Midwest that winter, speaking with renewed ardor on the meanings of Haymarket and Homestead.

Goldman returned to New York in December 1892 to find that life seemed empty without the camaraderie of the old commune. But she was not lonely for long. At a meeting of the committee working to free Berkman, she met Edward Brady, a dashing, well-educated anarchist who had just served 10 years in an Austrian jail for distributing forbidden pamphlets. Brady revived Goldman's childhood interest in literature, recommending that she read Goethe, Shakespeare, and Voltaire. Together they cultivated a wide circle of friends, most of whom frequented Justus Schwab's saloon, a gathering place for New York's radicals and the bohemian (unconventional) inhabitants of Greenwich Village. Goldman later noted that her friendship with Brady quickly "ripened into love," but illness soon tore her from her lover's arms. That spring, Goldman developed a mild case of tuberculosis. Doctors blamed her condition on the strain of her 60-hour workweek and urged her to rest. She left for Rochester, where under her sister Helena's devoted care her health gradually began to improve.

The industrial slump of 1893, which brought rampant unemployment and poverty to America's urban centers, drew the recovering Goldman back to New York. Dozens of progressive political groups there were struggling to relieve workers' distress, and Goldman hoped to join the fight. Ignoring ideological differences, she sought to ally herself with a number of organizations, especially those battling hunger and homelessness. Soon she found herself exhorting ever larger crowds of laborers to topple the political and economic

After her release from Blackwell's Island, Goldman met Ed Brady, a fellow radical who soon became her lover.

system that oppressed them. The legend of Red Emma was born that hectic summer when the young "high priestess of anarchy" went to jail for urging the jobless to take their bread from the rich.

Until she emerged from the dank cells of the Blackwell's Island prison, Goldman did not realize that the publicity surrounding her trial and incarceration had made her a celebrity. Fame, she quickly discovered, exacted a price. "The days and weeks that followed my release were like a nightmare," she wrote in *Living My Life*. "I needed quiet, peace, and privacy . . . but I was surrounded by people, and there were meetings nearly every evening." The conflict between her private needs and public obligations would long trouble Goldman, who believed the quest for personal fulfillment to be inseparable from political work.

Close relationships with fellow revolutionaries, Goldman felt, would foster a union of the personal and the political. For a time, she enjoyed this sort of companionship with Ed Brady. By writing a newspaper article on prisons, Goldman earned enough to allow the couple to move into their own four-room flat. Pleased with the arrangement, Brady asked Goldman to give up activism in order to settle down with him and have children. He saw child rearing as women's natural vocation and did not know that years earlier, Goldman had decided against motherhood. A child would have tied her down for years; it was unthinkable

to Goldman that she should compromise her dedication to the cause— especially while Berkman languished in prison. She refused Brady's request, writing later, "I had chosen my path; no man should ever take me from it."

Goldman chose instead to use the nursing skills she had acquired in prison to finance her career as a revolutionist. Against Brady's wishes, she took assignments as a practical nurse. She made a good living at the work, but Brady's displeasure eventually prompted her to quit nursing to start a business with him. They opened an ice cream parlor in Brooklyn, but it failed, convincing Brady that both he and Goldman would be better off if she resumed nursing. He urged her to get some formal schooling to increase her earning power. With the financial backing of Modest Stein, who was by now a successful commercial artist, Goldman decided to travel to Austria to earn a degree in nursing and midwifery.

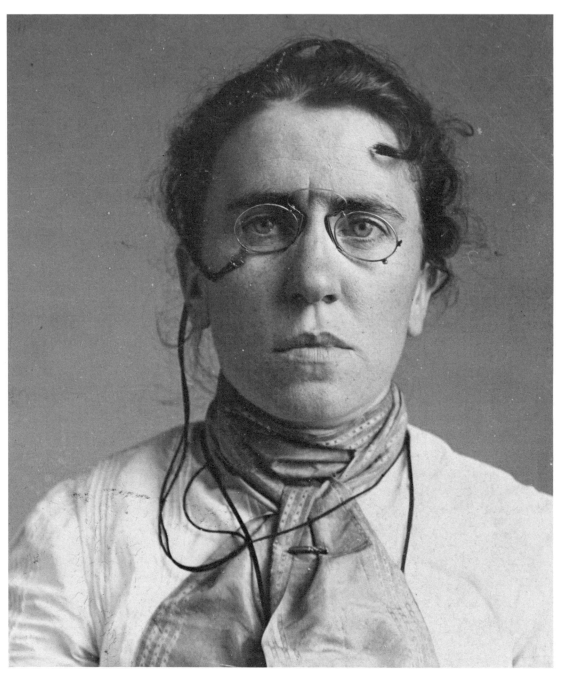

The first years of the 20th century proved difficult for Goldman.
Wrongly linked to the assassination of U.S. president William
McKinley, she was condemned by friends and enemies alike.

FOUR

Infamy and Misfortune

Emma Goldman sailed for Europe on August 15, 1895. Her trip began with a lecture tour in England, where her spirited speaking style and cleverness with hecklers brought her immediate popularity. While in London, Goldman enjoyed meeting some of her comrades in the worldwide movement, including Peter Kropotkin, one of the originators of anarchism. All too soon, though, it was time to move on. Goldman arrived in Vienna in October and, under the assumed name of Mrs. E. G. Brady, registered for nursing courses at the *Allgemeines Krankenhaus* (General Hospital).

Vienna fulfilled all of Goldman's expectations. The city was alive with cultural activity, and the young radical sought out its avant-garde, attending Richard Wagner's modern operas and the innovative plays of Gerhart Haupt-

mann and Henrik Ibsen. Lectures at school included a series by young Dr. Sigmund Freud, the pioneer of psychoanalysis. Hearing him speak, Goldman wrote, was like "being led out of a dark cellar into broad daylight."

Goldman reserved her greatest enthusiasm, however, for Friedrich Wilhelm Nietzsche, the renowned German philosopher-poet. Like the plays of Ibsen, Nietzsche's work seethed with the spirit of revolt—revolt not only against oppressive institutions but against the whole structure of conventional morality. Nietzsche dared to reject the narrow traditional values accepted without question by most Europeans and Americans. Thrilled to discover such a brilliant like-minded thinker, Goldman "longed to devour every line of his writings," she recalled. She read Nietzsche's radical philosophy into the

While on her way to Austria to study nursing and midwifery, Goldman stopped in London, England, to give some lectures and meet Peter Kropotkin, a founder of the anarchist movement.

small hours of the morning, sapping her daytime energy, "but what was physical strain in view of my raptures ...?" she wrote. It seemed to Goldman that Nietzsche was a truer anarchist than many of the revolutionaries she knew in New York.

Goldman's year abroad, away from her mentors, helped her refine her own understanding of anarchism. True liberty, in her view, required more than the overthrow of governments or the transfer of economic power to labor.

She came to believe that the rebel must attack not mere institutions but the "internal tyrants" of prejudice and superstition that supported them. While she studied in Europe, Goldman prepared to do battle with these evils in America. She was in for a long siege.

After earning her nursing and midwifery certificate, Goldman returned to the United States in November 1896. She resolved to "go on a tour ... study the country and its people, come close to the pulse of American life." To fund the trip she threw herself into nursing as well as delivering babies, all the while remaining active among the New York anarchists. Goldman coped well with the strenuous schedule; her jealous lover did not. Brady demanded that Goldman choose between their life together and her political work. When she refused to do so he moved out of their apartment. But they missed each other intensely and eventually reached a compromise in which Goldman agreed to curb what Ed Brady called her "mania for meetings." The lovers reunited, but their relationship continued to decay. Resentful of Brady's possessiveness and his efforts to harness her spirit, Goldman saw little reason to sacrifice her career. Though they continued to share a home, Goldman chose to spend nearly half of her time over the next two years on the road.

Goldman became the first woman anarchist to speak from coast to coast. On tour, her speaking virtuosity contributed to her growing fame. She attracted larger crowds than any other anarchist lecturer, in part because of her passionate, often fiery style. But just as intriguing to her listeners was her ability to challenge the beliefs of the majority, whether she attacked government or religion or defended workers' rights or women's rights. Although immigrant laborers remained her most loyal audience, Goldman occasionally spoke before American-born groups at fraternal lodges, philosophical societies, and even in churches.

Indeed, Goldman particularly enjoyed shocking listeners unfamiliar with her material. She liked, for instance, to urge suffragists (who sought the vote for women) and socialists (who often ran candidates for office) not to waste their efforts on the American electoral system. She delighted in exhorting patriots to oppose the Spanish-American War; in telling churchgoers that there is no God; and in astounding almost everyone by insisting on the right to freedom in sexual relations. When listeners objected to Goldman's outrageous assertions, she often returned quick, sarcastic salvos that kept her audiences in stitches.

Goldman cultivated a large audience outside the German-speaking anarchist community by making most of her speeches in near-perfect English. Lecturing in English, however, also attracted increasing numbers of the most unwelcome listeners: the police. Often, they stopped—or tried to stop—Goldman from delivering her message. For instance, in Providence, Rhode Island, in 1897 she was locked up before uttering a word. At the police station, she asked the sergeant in charge on what grounds she had been detained. "Because you're Emma Goldman," he answered. "Anarchists have no rights in this community, see?" In a pattern that would be repeated many times, Goldman was released the next morning and told by the mayor not to return to Providence. She usually scorned such advice and so ran into trouble again and again. Aware that she might be arrested at any time, Goldman always carried a book with her in case she needed to relieve the tedium of a night in jail.

In Vienna, Goldman discovered the work of the radical philosopher-poet Friedrich Nietzsche. "The beauty of his vision," she wrote, "carried me to undreamed-of heights."

American soldiers stand atop the bones of victims of the 1898 Spanish-American War. Goldman strenuously opposed the war and spoke out against it often.

Comrades everywhere invited the famous anarchist to stay in their homes. Such arrangements helped Goldman build a loose network of associates in dozens of cities. Some of these colleagues became lifelong friends and supporters. A brief affair with Max Baginski, a German-American anarchist living in Chicago, Illinois, established a bond that would last 40 years. Other relationships did not endure. When two midwestern fans offered Goldman financial backing for further medical studies, she seized the opportunity and sailed again for Europe in 1899. After a few months' agitation in England, she began vigorous work with the anarchists of Paris. Her American benefactors wrote to ask that she concentrate on school rather than politics, but in response Goldman fired back a letter. "E. G. the woman and her ideas are inseparable," she declared. "She does not exist for the amusement of upstarts, nor will she permit anyone to dictate to her. Keep your money." Accompanied by a new lover, radical journalist Hippolyte Havel, she returned to the United States in December 1900.

After another five months of nursing and participating in local meetings in New York, Goldman again left on tour, heading first for Cleveland, Ohio, and then for Chicago. She spent 11 weeks in the city where the Haymarket martyrs died, then traveled to Rochester for a summer vacation with her sisters and their families. On this occasion, Goldman noted, her "youthful friends"—her nieces, nephews, and brother Morris—made the holiday as stimulating as it was restful. "Tante Emma" told stories of her adventures and listened to the ideas and ambitions of her young admirers, much as she did with aspiring activists she met while on tour.

Unfortunately, Goldman's status as a role model for others caused her a great deal of trouble and anguish during the first years of the 20th century. On September 6, 1901, at the Buffalo, New York, fairgrounds, a young immigrant named Leon Czolgosz made his way through a crowd to fire a bullet into the chest of United States president William McKinley. Quickly arrested and questioned, Czolgosz claimed to be

Shortly after President William McKinley (standing at center of platform) addressed this crowd at the Buffalo, New York, fairgrounds, Leon Czolgosz shot him. Goldman was suspected of conspiring with the assassin.

an anarchist and a follower of Emma Goldman. Newspapers across the country published rumors of a Goldman-led conspiracy and called for her arrest. Eager to uncover a grand and evil plot behind Czolgosz's act, many Americans pointed to Goldman's association with Berkman, Henry Clay Frick's would-be assassin, and condemned her as a ringleader of anarchist terrorists.

In Chicago, several staunch Goldman supporters were held without bail while the authorities demanded her surrender. Goldman realized that her own arrest was inevitable and left for Chicago. Detectives took her into custody after she arrived in the Windy City and interrogated her for eight and a half hours, but they discovered nothing they could not already prove. Goldman barely knew Czolgosz. He had twice introduced himself to her—using another name—and had asked for reading material and information on the anarchist movement. The authorities could not charge Goldman with any crime, but they held her for two weeks anyway. Ironically, her incarceration may have been to her advantage, because she had received a number of death threats in the mail.

Official and popular frustration mounted when Czolgosz, despite repeated beatings by police, refused to implicate Goldman. He maintained that she knew nothing of the act he said he performed "for the American people." Goldman in turn refused to condemn Czolgosz, remarking that such terrorists are lost souls with correct motives, if not acceptable meth-

Goldman did not approve of McKinley's murder, but she defended Czolgosz as a "supersensitive being" driven to the act by outside forces. Most of her anarchist colleagues rejected her position.

ods. She further shocked the public by offering her nursing skills to both the jailed man (who had been beaten by the police) and the injured president. But McKinley soon died, and his assassin was quickly tried and executed. Goldman's ambivalence regarding Czolgosz's violent deed did little for her reputation or the image of the anarchist movement. A wave of arrests and anti-anarchist mob violence swept the nation.

Many anarchists, fearing for their safety, rushed to denounce Czolgosz. But even though Berkman's Homestead attentat had convinced Goldman that murder should not be used for political ends, she felt disgusted with her cowardly comrades. She stubbornly spoke of Czolgosz as a martyr. Political assassins, she insisted, were "driven to some violent expression, even at the sacrifice of their own lives, because they cannot supinely [passively] witness the misery and suffering of their fellows. The blame for such acts must be laid at the door of those who are responsible for the injustice and inhumanity which dominate the world."

Goldman's stance reflected much more than her political theories. The rash act committed by Czolgosz paralleled that committed by Berkman nine years earlier. To abandon Czolgosz would be to abandon Berkman, a move Goldman simply could not make. In her autobiography, Goldman related how the face of Czolgosz haunted her for months after his execution, precisely as the image of Berkman had after his conviction. She felt a deep sense of guilt over both episodes, for she shared the motives of both men and had even inspired them, yet she had escaped the dire punishment occasioned by their actions. Now, most of her colleagues condemned the kind of dedication Goldman most admired. Even Berkman, in a 1901 message from prison, belittled Czolgosz and himself for failing to awaken "the popular mind." Goldman sank into deep despair.

Vilified in the press and ostracized by her former colleagues, Goldman found it impossible to speak in public or publish her work. To make matters worse, Ed Brady died suddenly and mysteriously, heightening Goldman's sense of isolation and hopelessness. She would receive little sympathy during her time of grief. An undesirable tenant, she was forced to move frequently because landlords and neighbors inevitably discovered her identity. She managed to get work as a night nurse, but she avoided political functions, where she was invariably unwelcome. By the summer of 1902 she yearned for activity and resolved to put her months of depression behind her. Events fortuitously allowed her to do just that.

An attempted revolt and the repression that followed shook czarist Russia, reviving a spirit of common cause among New York's radicals and reestablishing Goldman's place in the community. She first turned her attention to a strike of 140,000 coal miners that had started in the spring. Mine owners—the railroads—refused to recognize a union or improve conditions in company-owned mining towns. Goldman undertook a tour of the coal mining region and the Midwest that included more than one arrest "on general principles," as she put it. "You're Emma Goldman, aren't you? That's enough!" one police sergeant explained to her.

The antianarchist hysteria of 1901 and 1902 culminated in the passage of several state laws, such as New York State's Criminal Anarchy Act, that made it a felony to advocate assassination or the overthrow of the government. The U.S. Congress also took

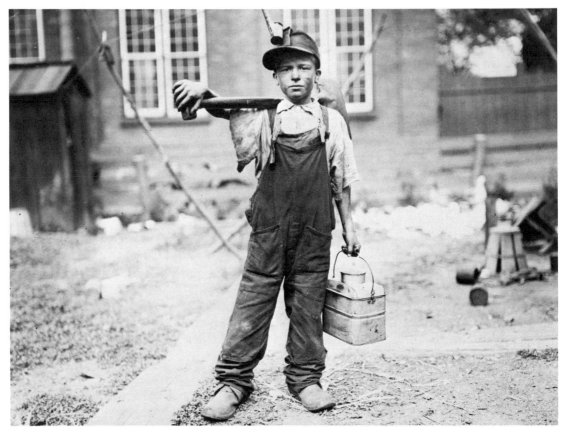

A seven-year-old mine worker takes a break from his grueling day. Goldman lectured throughout America's mining region during the 1902 coal miners' strike.

steps against radicals: A 1903 federal immigration law barred entrance to anyone "who disbelieves in or is opposed to all organized governments," or who had any affiliation with anarchist organizations. This statute, upheld by the U.S. Supreme Court, supplied the government with the means to prosecute and deport many radicals. Such measures, however, were hardly necessary to quell anarchism in this country.

At a time when labor, business, and the federal government appeared to vie for control of America, most ordinary citizens craved law and order. The anarchist ideal of a world without laws struck most people as a useless if not dangerous fantasy. The ranks of American anarchists never numbered more than tens of thousands, compared with those of socialists and trade unionists, who gained millions of sympathizers in the early years of the 20th century.

Except that they believed large government could be good government, Goldman agreed with many of the short- and long-term social goals of these other activists. In the years to come, she followed both conscience and common sense by identifying herself with radical causes apart from anarchism.

Indeed, although often portrayed as an uncompromising extremist, Goldman regarded the flowering of non-anarchist radicalism optimistically, regularly offering various groups her energetic cooperation. As a mobilizer of support for the new Russian revolutionaries, she wrote, she "hobnobbed with respectability," gladly accepting invitations to speak before such upper-class groups as the Manhattan Liberal Club. When a British anarchist named John Turner was jailed upon arriving in America, Goldman quietly enlisted the support of influential liberals for a ncw Free Speech League. During these years she did some of her most effective work under the alias of Miss E. G. Smith.

Goldman's low-profile strategy released her from the burden imposed by the notoriety that both her name and the anarchist movement had attained in America. This new freedom enabled her to seek fulfillment of her liberationist vision through involvement in broader political movements and cultural activities. Her vision of revolution now centered around the elimination of repressive social values, a goal she felt could be attained through education. Goldman had come to believe that no better teacher existed than

The cover of the first issue of Goldman's magazine, Mother Earth, *reflects the idealism of the anarchist movement. The journal was published between 1906 and 1917.*

the modern theater, in which playwrights and actors often portrayed the tragedy of the contemporary struggles for power in personal relationships and in society. Acting on this conviction, Goldman served as manager and translator for a Russian theatrical troupe in late 1905. Audiences, she later recalled, loved their productions of European

Women sew piecework in their slum apartment. A champion of both the feminist and labor movements, Goldman was particularly concerned with the welfare of working women.

plays that displayed "the terrible diseases of our social body." The experience confirmed Goldman's understanding of anarchism: Rather than a specific program of political reform, it was the effort to achieve freedom in everyday life.

With a renewed sense of mission Goldman decided to publish a magazine to spread her notion of "the liberating ideal." She used funds donated by the theater troupe and recruited Max Baginski to help edit the magazine. They put out the first issue of *Mother Earth* in March 1906. On the front cover of the publication were depicted a man and a woman, freed from chains, facing a sunrise. Inside were articles on anarchist theory, news about radical circles, a poem, and a short story. Without question, the most powerful piece was an essay that was contributed by Goldman.

In "The Tragedy of Woman's Emancipation" Goldman took issue with the women's movement of her time. She was convinced that the American movement had lost sight of its original goals. Contemporary feminist activists who campaigned for the right to vote and work outside the home sought, in Goldman's view, mere "external emancipation." True freedom, she felt, was not such a simple matter. "How much independence is gained," she wrote, "if the narrowness and lack of freedom of the home is exchanged for the narrowness and lack of freedom of the factory, sweatshop, department store, or office?" According to Goldman, women could not free themselves in a world where working *men* were enslaved, especially since women earned even lower wages.

Women would be liberated not only by reform in the workplace, Goldman argued, but by a revolution in relationships between the sexes. Most women of her time could not support themselves financially unless they married. Social customs that limited women to domestic roles denied them economic and political power, allowing men to keep them in a subordinate position. Marriage for many was thus transformed into a purely economic arrangement in which one member was completely dependent upon the other. "The narrow, materialistic confines of marriage as it is speedily crush the tender flower of affection," lamented Goldman. She believed that, although they attained a level of economic security, most married women lost their individuality. They were defined not as people but as objects who served their husbands and children. Goldman believed that few women forced to marry out of economic necessity were truly happy. Neither men nor women would be free, she argued, until all personal relationships were founded on mutual love and respect rather than on tradition or financial need.

Goldman's article further asserted that both men and women had to overcome certain deep-rooted beliefs about themselves. She criticized those who considered women men's moral superiors as well as those who held that

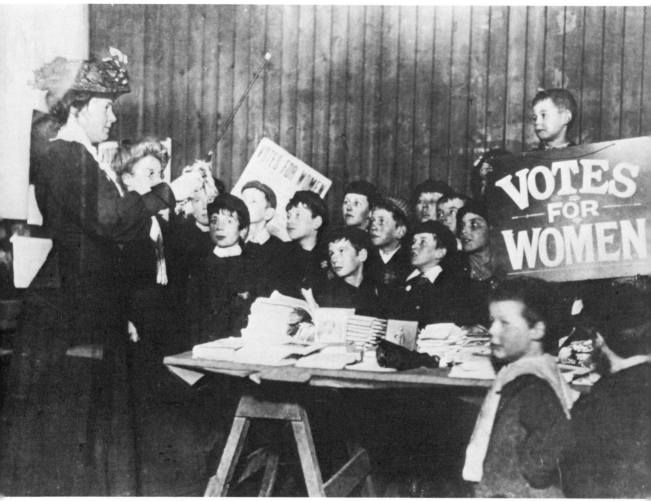

Schoolchildren learn a feminist song. During the early years of the 20th century, the women's movement focused on winning the vote for women, a goal Goldman considered shortsighted.

women were essentially evil. True liberation would come to women, Goldman insisted, only when women were accepted as men's spiritual equals. "Since woman's greatest misfortune has been that she was looked upon as either angel or devil," she wrote, "her true salvation lies in being placed on earth." Goldman's assertions regarding the power of society's traditional attitudes toward women, and her insistence that "true emancipation begins in a woman's [own] soul," anticipated the feminists of the later 20th century.

Her words have since inspired countless people striving for equality of the sexes.

Goldman empathized personally with women who risked financial and emotional security by choosing to live a life outside the traditional realms. At the age of 37, her own dedication to the world beyond marriage and motherhood continued to frustrate her in her search to combine financial security with personal fulfillment. In the *Mother Earth* venture and her growing popularity as a public speaker she saw the possibility of supporting herself through the work she loved. She soon retired her nurse's uniform, vowing that E. G. Smith would be no more. Determined to succeed, Emma Goldman set her sights on "the open road."

In her late forties and early fifties Goldman reached a broad audience through Mother Earth *and her many speaking tours.*

FIVE

The Queen of Anarchy

After the first issue of *Mother Earth* was printed and mailed, Goldman prepared for her customary spring lecture tour. The new magazine's monthly readership would average between 3,000 and 8,000, but sales to the small, loyal following could not finance the entire operation. As a result, Goldman's speaking tours had to serve as fund-raising expeditions. Nonetheless, Goldman had little time to think about *Mother Earth*'s financial woes that year. Alexander Berkman was to be freed from prison on the 18th of May, 1906.

Goldman cut her tour short to meet Berkman on the evening of his release. She was shocked by her friend's gaunt and distraught appearance, and distressed that neither company nor solitude seemed to put him at ease. After a round of celebratory meetings Gold-

man and Berkman traveled to her new farm—a gift from wealthy New York activist Bolton Hall—near Ossining, New York. Goldman's renowned Jewish cooking helped replace some of Berkman's lost flesh, but the retreat failed to restore his spirits. The old comrades returned to the brownstone at 210 East 13th Street, which housed Goldman's apartment and the *Mother Earth* office.

In prison, Berkman had revised some of his severe revolutionary thinking, but in many ways he still lived in 1892. He still thought of Goldman as his "sailor girl" rather than as the foremost anarchist in America. Haunted by nightmares and depressed by inactivity, he criticized Goldman's new friends and new ideas. Goldman in turn expected their old romance to rekindle but smothered it by overwhelming her "boy" with worried attention. Only after Berkman resumed work as a labor activist and became a coeditor of *Mother Earth* were he and Goldman able to make the difficult readjustment.

Against the wishes of many supporters, the magazine's October 1906 issue memorialized Czolgosz, McKinley's assassin, on the fifth anniversary of his execution. The editors' decision cost *Mother Earth* many subscribers and attracted some unwanted attention. A new "anarchist squad" of New York Police Department detectives initiated a crackdown on radical activity in the city. They intimidated hall owners, discouraging them from renting to anarchists, and arrested Goldman and several others at a Czolgosz memorial meeting.

The disapproval of comrades and attacks by the authorities only strengthened Goldman's desire to be heard. *Mother Earth* increasingly became a vehicle for her own voice, publicizing her lecture dates and printing her reports from "On Tour." In addition to being Goldman's personal newsletter, *Mother Earth* sold books and pamphlets on social theory and modern literature and mobilized support for radicals under fire. Many would-be contributors were put off by the magazine's strident politics, so the journal relied on Goldman's longtime associates for most of its articles. But despite its troubles, *Mother Earth* remained the only nationally distributed English-language anarchist magazine in the United States.

Over the years, the *Mother Earth* office became a fixture of the avant-garde culture of downtown New York. For a decade, Goldman, when not on tour, could be found presiding over a whirl of activity at the building known simply as "210." In *Living My Life* she recalled, "My room was the living room, dining room, and *Mother Earth* office, all in one." Comrades wandered in and out of the house at all hours. When not swamped with work, Goldman enjoyed the gaiety and camaraderie of this community of self-proclaimed nonconformists.

One of these rebels was Hutchins Hapgood, a journalist who was among the first to chronicle the life of the immigrant poor. He referred affectionately to the *Mother Earth* enclave as "the home of lost dogs." Another frequent visitor was William D. "Big Bill" Haywood, guiding light of the Industrial Workers of the World (IWW), a radical labor organization known as the "Wobblies." He waxed poetic over Goldman's coffee, which he said was "black as the night, strong as the revolutionary ideal, sweet as love." The *Mother Earth* circle sponsored weekly discussions and some very lively social events. At one of the annual New Year's Eve parties, Goldman came dressed as a nun and cleared the dance floor for a rendition of a dance she called the "Anarchist's slide."

The economic needs of the magazine and its "family" kept Goldman on the road at least six months out of each year. Her local and cross-country tours of 1907 and 1908 established the pattern for these trips. Before arriving in

The lively radical community that formed around the Mother Earth *collective included Big Bill Haywood (above), leader of the Industrial Workers of the World (IWW).*

Attendance averaged several hundred persons per appearance; in larger towns Goldman generally stayed for more than one meeting.

Goldman retreated for at least an hour of solitude before speaking, to collect her thoughts and battle with stage fright. More and more often, she spoke before a variety of diffcrent audiences in each city. She addressed everyone from well-to-do matrons at women's associations to immigrant Jewish laborers who lightened the rigors of travel, she recalled, "with their usual Semitic warmth." Tailoring her approach to each group, Goldman was praised for both the reason and the passion of her presentations. And everywhere the police came out, intimidating listeners and sometimes even banning appearances of the "Red Queen"—a strategy that sometimes backfircd.

In March of 1908, after a successful series of meetings in St. Louis, Goldman proceeded to Chicago, where police ordered all halls closed to anarchists. When she attempted to speak unannounced at a rally for the unemployed, a police officer grabbed her and pulled her from the platform. "The police are here to cause another Haymarket riot. Don't give them the chance," Goldman called out to the audience. "Walk out quietly and you will help our cause a thousand times more." The crowd cheered and left singing.

After reports of this extraordinary incident circulated, influential Chicagoans wrote letters to the newspapers,

each city, Goldman sent ahead a list of lecture topics, which ranged from "The Real Meaning of Anarchy" to "The Revolutionary Spirit in Modern Drama" to "Woman Under Anarchism." Local comrades distributed notices of the lectures and advertised when possible in newspapers. All employed persons paid admission of a nickel or dime, and anarchist literature was sold to raise additional money.

Alexander Berkman (in spectacles) leads a 1908 rally in New York's Union Square. He and Goldman spent much of their time addressing similar crowds throughout the nation.

protesting the abridgement of free speech. One of the local dailies printed Goldman's protest message and her call for the formation of a free speech league. Goldman considered the publicity "splendid advertising," for it brought thousands to hear her in Milwaukee, Wisconsin, and Minneapolis, Minnesota. But the constant turmoil that surrounded her eventually took its toll. Often, train rides between stops provided Goldman with her only escape from "the strain and stress of meetings, discussions, and debates." She felt afflicted by a disturbing "inner void" and suffered at least one collapse attributed to fatigue and depression.

More than ever, Goldman felt lonely amid the crowds of admirers and detractors.

The solution to Goldman's loneliness seemed to arrive in the flamboyant form of Dr. Ben L. Reitman, well-known "king" of the Chicago hobos. After spending his youth wandering about the United States and Europe, Reitman had returned to his native city and found work. With the help of his employer, a famous surgeon, he entered and graduated medical school. Afterward, Reitman maintained his connections to society's marginal men and women, organizing a "hobo college" and leading protests of the unem-

Ben Reitman (at head of table) attends a "hobo banquet" in 1907. When he met Goldman the following year, he was immediately attracted to the fiery activist.

ployed. From their first meeting, during Goldman's 1908 Chicago appearance, Reitman admired the renowned anarchist speaker. Nine years Goldman's junior, the ruggedly handsome, thoroughly unconventional Reitman fascinated her. She agreed to allow him to join her on tour.

The hobo king wanted to make himself useful, and he soon displayed an impressive talent for drumming up publicity and running meetings. As the months passed he became invaluable. Reitman's skills as a manager increased attendance and pamphlet sales at Goldman's lectures, thus paying his expenses and helping to fund the publication of *Mother Earth*. Just as important, Reitman's amorous attentions cheered and revitalized Goldman, restoring her joy in her work. She believed she had found "someone who would love the woman in me and yet who would also be able to share my work." But, as she would later reflect, it was not her fate to have harmony in love. Goldman's letters to Reitman and other friends reveal the heights of ecstasy and depths of despair that accompanied her growing emotional dependency on Reitman.

One source of anguish was her new lover's affairs with other women. Reitman repeatedly gave in to temptation

Butte mont.

Emma GOLDMAN

LECTURES
AT THE AUDITORIUM JUNE
24th
1912
TO·NIGHT SUBJECT·Why the poor
Should not have children.

Goldman relied on Reitman's personal support and public relations skills during her long speaking tours. Here, Reitman (center) helps publicize one of Goldman's birth control lectures.

when separated from Goldman, only to confess and ask her forgiveness later. Goldman's understandable jealousy especially grieved her because she had always believed that relations between men and women should be grounded in complete freedom for both partners. Another trouble spot in Goldman's relationship with Reitman was his lack of commitment to radical politics and avant-garde culture. Most of the *Mother Earth* group shared these inter-

ests and perceived Reitman as shallow. Despite the conflicts, Goldman wrote that Reitman remained "the most compelling element in my life."

Whatever the cost, Reitman satisfied vital needs in Goldman. Their relationship, which lasted until the end of 1916, coincided with Goldman's period of greatest productivity and importance. During these years she wrote more essays, gave more lectures, and attracted larger crowds than ever before. In addition to working as a political activist, Goldman developed a reputation as a perceptive social critic. "There are many good articles in the Goldman creed," one mainstream newspaper reported. "The trouble with this extraordinary woman is that she is a revolutionist, instead of an evolutionist. . . . She cannot see the great advancement since yesterday." But Goldman could not alter her views on the question of social upheaval. "No real social change has ever come about without a revolution," she insisted. "Never can a new idea move within the law."

Like other American proponents of change, Goldman pointed to the nation's revolutionary origins as proof of her claims. She often declared that real American patriotism meant a deep concern for liberty. For the most part, the government considered her views dangerous and tried to keep them from spreading. In one such attempt, hundreds of police surrounded thousands of listeners at a Goldman lecture on patriotism in San Francisco. After her speech denouncing militarism, a uniformed soldier named William Buwalda approached the platform and shook her hand, only to be arrested, court-martialed, and sentenced to five years in military prison. He was pardoned at the president's request 10 months later, but the incident, in Goldman's view, proved that patriotism itself had become "a menace to liberty." Popular patriotism, "like all insatiable monsters, demands all or nothing," she wrote. "It does not admit that a soldier

is also a human being, who has a right to his own feelings and opinions, his own inclinations and ideas."

There is no doubt that Goldman's criticisms of patriotism, capitalism, government, religion, and marriage offended multitudes of American citizens. Her extremism, in the opinion of some, justified silencing. But attempts at suppression brought sympathy from others and prompted the press to report Goldman's exploits with greater fairness. The *New York World* paid Goldman $250 for an essay entitled "What I Believe." The editor of the *St. Louis Mirror* published a laudatory profile that concluded "there is nothing wrong with Miss Goldman's gospel that I can see, except this: She is about eight thousand years ahead of her time." This kind of publicity helped counter Goldman's original image as a demagogue interested only in the destruction of the existing order.

Goldman helped transform her image by turning her attention to more popular topics. Her campaign for freedom of expression, for instance, won her many supporters. In her view, the United States did not live up to its own "paper guarantees" of liberty. "Free speech," she wrote, "means the unlimited right of expression, or nothing at all." One did not have to accept Goldman's more radical ideas to agree with her interpretation of the Bill of Rights. Some Americans backed up their new opinion of Goldman with action. For instance, when New York police broke up one of her public lectures on the plays of Ibsen, a wealthy oilman promised her the use of the barn on his country estate.

Goldman's lessons on the importance of civil liberty were lost on government officials determined to stop the "Queen of Anarchy." The U.S. Postal Service gave in to pressure applied by Anthony Comstock, president of the powerful New York Society for the Suppression of Vice, and refused to deliver an issue of *Mother Earth* that contained a Goldman essay on the causes of prostitution. Worse, the Bureau of Immigration revoked the citizenship papers of Goldman's former husband, thus rendering her a resident alien. Goldman was forced to cancel a trip to Australia that she had planned to make with Reitman. If she had left the country, she would have been barred from returning.

Such attacks—and Goldman's response to them—underlined her independence and her willingness to risk all for the sake of her cause. Equating herself with the very spirit of liberty, she asserted in the pages of *Mother Earth* that the government "might as well attempt to direct the course of the stars as to direct the course of my life's work." A growing number of sympathizers agreed. In the years preceding World War I, Goldman attracted many followers from among the young intellectuals who flocked to the cities. New York's Greenwich Village seethed with political and cultural activity during that period, and its cafés were filled with rebellious young bohemians who looked up to Goldman as a role model.

One of those rebels was socialist poet and editor Floyd Dell, who wrote that Goldman "has a legitimate social function, that of holding before our eyes the ideal of freedom." Roger Baldwin, a young lawyer who would go on to found the American Civil Liberties Union, likened his first contact with Goldman to a religious conversion: "It was the eye opener of my life. Never before had I heard such social passion, such courageous exposure of basic evils, such electric power behind words, such a sweeping challenge to all the values I had been taught to hold dear. From that day forth I was her admirer."

Success among this small but active minority inspired Goldman to change her strategy as an activist. After 20 years' work in radical causes, she had concluded that those she termed the "intelligent minorities," and not the masses, carried the banner of progress. "I prefer to reach the few who really want to learn," she wrote in the preface to her book *Anarchism and Other Essays*, published in 1910, "rather than the many who come to be amused" by a well-known speaker. She hoped to "plant the seeds of thought" that would turn the complacency of educated people into activism. Some of her anarchist friends disagreed with her new approach. Berkman, for one, still held that it was most important to reach those who were most oppressed—the workers.

But Goldman believed it vital to participate in the broad, growing cultural movement that was striving to liberate the individual from stifling social customs. America was different than Russia, she asserted, and so its revolution should be different. In the United States, Goldman noted, the people themselves upheld the tyrannies of government and the "standards of respectability." No revolution could occur, she reasoned, unless the "intellectual proletarians"—educated, middle-class people who worked with their minds rather than their hands—understood that the capitalist system controlled

Striking mill workers confront U.S. soldiers in Lawrence, Massachusetts, in 1912. The early 20th century was a time of great conflict between organized labor and business owners.

Elizabeth Gurley Flynn (right), an IWW leader, played a key role in the Paterson, New Jersey, silk mill strike of 1913. She and Goldman were but two of many women active in radical causes.

others. When other radicals accused her of being a mere entertainer, Goldman defended her methods. She told her critics that, while some reformers focused solely on the form government should take, she attacked the whole system of "acquired prejudices and superstitions" that supported oppressive governments. She had found that plays could reach people as theory could not—with concrete examples of social wrongs. In 1914, this conviction inspired her to collect her drama lectures and publish them in a volume entitled *The Social Significance of Modern Drama.*

Goldman found another outlet for her interest in education in the Modern School movement. Inspired by the theories of Francisco Ferrer, a Spanish anarchist and educator, the movement advocated a progressive school system. Modern School advocates believed in education that promoted individual growth in children rather than conformity to a single pattern. They hoped to establish schools where learning was based on individual aptitude instead of rote memorization. In Greenwich Village, a Ferrer Center for adult education offered free lectures by artists and scholars; eventually, supporters sponsored several schools for youngsters. As with many of Goldman's beliefs, the initially unpopular ideas of the Modern School educators would be widely accepted only much later.

The labor movement, however, still claimed the majority of Goldman's time. In 1912 and 1913, layoffs and wage cuts provoked massive strikes in

and limited their lives as much as it did the lives of factory workers.

In order to illustrate her ideas, Goldman often linked her social criticism to examples from literature. The approach appealed both to her intellectual followers and to laborers. In fact, her most popular talks on the 1912 tour focused on the revolutionary message in modern drama. Goldman was among the first to bring the "new" theater to the American public, helping to popularize the work of George Bernard Shaw, August Strindberg, Anton Chekhov, and

The wounds of these San Diego activists attest to the mob violence directed against radicals there. Unintimidated, Goldman and Reitman visited the city in 1912.

Lawrence, Massachusetts, and Paterson, New Jersey. Once again business leaders refused to negotiate with the unions. They defended their stance by claiming labor organizations were linked to such incidents as the recent uprisings in Mexico and the bombing of the *Los Angeles Times* building. Warned to stay away from San Diego, where vigilantes had attacked members of the IWW, Goldman and Reitman arrived anyway in May 1912, only to be pursued by a mob. Goldman was restricted to her hotel room by the chief of police while Reitman was seized, beaten, stripped, tarred, and abandoned outside town. The publicity and sympathy generated in the East and Midwest by this horrifying event did nothing to slow the government's campaign against Goldman. The incident heralded a new phase of Goldman's career, during which her rising fame and influence prompted drastic measures on the part of her great enemy, the state.

Goldman exhorts a crowd of Union Square demonstrators to action in 1916. Even when threatened with arrest, imprisonment, and deportation, she fearlessly carried on her crusade.

S I X

"The Habit of Rebellion"

The arrival of the new year, 1914, did not bring better times to the American workplace. Unemployment continued to rise, and in the atmosphere of dissatisfaction Goldman's lectures gained popularity. Especially well received were those on literature: Audiences apparently enjoyed learning about art and social problems simultaneously. Goldman's weekly New York meetings were attended by a virtual cult of followers, many of them more interested in the woman herself than in any of her causes. The lectures brought together a community of generally young cultural radicals. Speech topics varied, but the themes of personal liberation and social improvement provided a foundation for all the discussions. Collections were taken up to help the poor, whose plight was blamed on the wealthy (who exploited them) and the government (which ignored them). Whatever the motivations of her audience, Goldman continued to deliver the message that in capitalism and the authoritarian systems wedded to it lay the roots of most present and past suffering.

Events seemed to bear out Goldman's views. When a young anarchist named Frank Tannenbaum led a crowd of jobless people to a Fifth Avenue church to ask for assistance, the presiding pastor had him arrested and prosecuted. Later that year, the Colorado Fuel and Iron Company evicted striking miners from company housing. The protesters set up makeshift quarters with their families, but the company set their tents afire; 19 died in what came to be known as the Ludlow Massacre. Once again Goldman responded with a speaking tour while Alexander Berkman organized demonstrations.

A striking miner retrieves the body of a fellow protester after the Ludlow Massacre of 1914. Such outrages always galvanized Goldman into action.

In the wake of the Ludlow Massacre, several New York anarchists manufactured a bomb, probably intending to deposit it on the doorstep of John D. Rockefeller, the owner of the Colorado Fuel and Iron Company. Instead, the weapon exploded in their Lexington Avenue apartment building, killing four. Political activists held a tremendous public memorial service at which Berkman offered glowing eulogies of the dead radicals. The event further tarnished the general public's image of

anarchists. Under Berkman's direction, the July 1914 issue of *Mother Earth* carried articles praising the "martyrs" and calls to violence by several who had never been associated with the magazine or Goldman before. Goldman, away on tour, was furious. Opposed to violence, she had always managed to keep *Mother Earth* free of "such language." She was again forced to choose between condoning violence and condemning her comrades. Goldman chose not to criticize them publicly, but the gap between her own methods and those of other anarchists continued to widen.

Leaving the *Mother Earth* incident behind, Goldman carried on her crusade for a revolution in values. She now focused on American attitudes toward sexuality, becoming one of the first public speakers to discuss such controversial issues as the position of homosexuals in society. She decried the "social ostracism" that homosexuals endured and denounced such injustices as the imprisonment of British writer Oscar Wilde, jailed for homosexuality. Goldman proposed greater tolerance and understanding, but her arguments usually fell on deaf ears, even among fellow radicals. More successful was her continuing campaign to promote birth control.

As a nurse, Goldman had seen destitute immigrants, ignorant of ways to limit their offspring, struggling to raise more children than their incomes could support. Laws dating from the 19th century made it illegal to teach birth control practices, so Goldman limited herself to general talks and articles on the need to choose contraception. But when an old protégée, Margaret Sanger, began to experience legal trouble, Goldman decided to take action. Sanger, the pioneer of the birth control movement, authored frank pamphlets on sex, such as "What Every Girl Should Know" and the new journal, *Woman Rebel*. The authorities attempted to suppress her ideas and arrested her at least once. Believing that she too should "share the consequences" of birth control ag-

itation, in March 1915, Goldman initiated a lecture series on "Family Limitation" that included specific information on the use of contraceptives. Surprisingly, she was not arrested until almost a year later, at a rally in New York's Carnegie Hall. By then, birth control was a national issue, and Goldman considered the publicity generated by her trial well worth the 15 days she spent in the county workhouse.

Eager to speak out on nearly every controversial issue, Goldman earned fervent admiration from the nation's

Birth control activist Margaret Sanger reads an issue of the Blast. *Sanger's courage in the face of persecution inspired Goldman to take up the birth control cause.*

radical minority and equally passionate animosity from the mainstream public. Her stand on militarism inspired particularly intense reactions on both sides. No one could ignore the implications of the European conflict that had broken out in 1914 and escalated into World War I, a vast clash of two powerful alliances. A growing number of Americans sympathized with England, France, Russia, and some of the smaller European states in their struggle against the combined forces of Germany, Italy, and Austria-Hungary. Concerned about the struggle's outcome, many—including the United States government—urged that the nation prepare for war. Many other Americans, however, felt strongly that the nation should, at all costs, avoid being drawn into the brawl.

From the beginning, Goldman attracted attention with her War on War. She characterized the European situation as a fight between capitalists bent on making their nations rich through conquest. Hoping to encourage her adopted country to stay out of the fray, Goldman began making speeches against the doctrine of preparedness. In a lecture entitled "Preparedness: The Road to Universal Slaughter," she contended that investment in arms always leads to war—and to the suppression of liberty in the name of military necessity.

Hoping to further the War on War, Goldman left for a speaking tour in 1916 while her lover, Ben Reitman, served a 60-day jail term for handing out birth control pamphlets. When she visited California she reunited with Berkman and fellow anarchist Eleanor Fitzgerald, who had moved to San Francisco together to edit an anarchist labor paper called *The Blast*. That city witnessed, in one week, both a government-sponsored "preparedness" and a Goldman-led "antipreparedness" meeting. At the government's rally, a bomb exploded, causing 48 casualties. Without any evidence, authorities pinned the crime on labor organizer Thomas Mooney and several of his associates. Months of protest work by Goldman and Berkman on behalf of the accused helped generate national and international outrage and rescued Mooney from death row.

The burden of carrying on her various struggles gradually began to fatigue the 47-year-old Goldman. The intensification of these battles coincided with a realization that her relationship with Reitman had come to an end. The hobo doctor talked of settling down and having children; long rebuffed by the activist, he married another woman early in 1917. "I felt unutterably weary and possessed only of a desire to get away somewhere and forget the failure of my personal life," Goldman remarked in her autobiography. She managed to escape from her obligations and travel to Provincetown, Massachusetts. There, she enjoyed the soothing company of her niece Stella Comminsky Ballantine, Max Baginski, and her friends from Greenwich Village—Hutchins Hapgood, radical journalist John Reed, and other writers active in the experimental theater movement. After a rest-

U.S. secretary of war Newton Baker draws a number in the World War I military draft. As a critic of the entire war effort, Goldman was particularly opposed to the draft.

ful month, she heeded Berkman's call back into battle.

In March 1917, Woodrow Wilson was inaugurated for a second term as president of the United States. His election campaign had appealed to voters who did not want the nation to get involved in the European conflict and had relied on such slogans as He Kept Us Out of War. But the country had been arming itself, and both alliances had rejected Wilson's proposals for a negotiated peace. Meanwhile, a desperate Germany conducted unrestricted submarine assaults on supply ships—including American vessels—in the Atlantic Ocean. That spring the U.S. Congress declared war against the ma-

rauding German and Austrian empires. The Selective Service Act instituted the draft, and America prepared to send 2 million of its young men to fight "the war to end all wars."

In the ensuing months Goldman saw the antiwar movement virtually vanish before her eyes. In its place arose new intolerance for those who opposed the country's war effort. Now, anyone who objected to American participation in the war, along with all German Americans, regardless of their political beliefs, could suffer damaging accusations of disloyalty. Goldman grieved that America, "a country where it is as possible to rationally separate races as it is possible to unscramble scrambled eggs," should turn against its newer citizens, most of whom were at least as patriotic as the descendants of the colonists. She claimed that her own love of America and its promise of liberty in fact compelled her to speak out against the war—and all wars. "Our patriotism," she would later tell a jury, "is that of a man who loves a woman with open eyes. He is enchanted by her beauty, yet sees her faults. So we too love America."

Feminists stage an antiwar protest in 1915, when popular opposition to the war was widespread. After the U.S. entered the conflict, pacifist sentiments were frowned upon.

In May 1917, Berkman, Goldman, and others of the *Mother Earth* circle formed a "No-Conscription League" dedicated to conscientious opposition to the draft. Its first rally, in New York, drew over 8,000 people. Goldman then left on a brief tour to found antidraft leagues in other cities. The June issue of *Mother Earth* also focused on the draft. Its cover, emblazoned with the headline IN MEMORIAM—AMERICAN DEMOCRACY, criticized the government for not allowing the public to vote on the draft. The magazine contained an anticonscription manifesto written by Berkman and Goldman. The document was reprinted in many newspapers and distributed as a leaflet by the tens of thousands.

A June 4th antidraft meeting in New York City drew the largest crowd yet, a mixture of police, soldiers, and sympathizers. When a soldier stood and called for the silencing of Berkman, Goldman singlehandedly prevented a riot by urging her enraged supporters to leave peacefully. At the next rally, police arrested young men who did not carry draft registration cards. Finally, on June 15th, the U.S. marshal for New York burst into the *Mother Earth* office. Detectives ransacked the files while Goldman and Berkman were taken away to prison and charged with conspiracy to obstruct the draft.

The defendants resolved to plead their own case in court. During the trial, Goldman insisted that neither she nor Berkman had ever counseled anyone not to register. The prosecution falsely and irrelevantly claimed that the anarchists had advocated the violent overthrow of the government and disobedience to all laws. The defense, in turn, called witnesses to refute the charge. But the state dismissed these efforts. "[Goldman] is a menace to our well-ordered institutions," contended the district attorney, and the press agreed. The *New York Times* wrote that "leniency would be out of place." With little hope of acquittal, Goldman and Berkman used their time in court to deliver speeches in defense of their ideas. Goldman was especially eloquent, passionately defending her right of free speech and criticizing those who would limit it to views deemed "within the law."

The jury took less than an hour to reach a verdict. Goldman and Berkman were found guilty. Judge Julius Mayer handed down the maximum sentence of 2 years in prison and fines of $10,000 each, recommending that the defendants be forced to leave the country at the end of their prison terms. The two anarchists spent the next several weeks in federal prison while Harry Weinberger, their legal adviser, secured an appeal before the Supreme Court.

Goldman was freed on bail, but Berkman remained in prison. The San Francisco attorney general had called him to stand trial for the 1916 Preparedness Day bombing, and his friends feared that he would be seized by California state agents if released. Goldman spearheaded a successful fight to quash the extradition and allow Berkman to leave prison on bail. She also continued to speak out against the draft and limita-

Socialist leader and presidential candidate Eugene Debs was sentenced to 10 years in prison under the 1917 Espionage Act. While in prison, he ran for president for a fifth time.

tions on free speech, using her lectures to raise funds for other imprisoned activists as well as for her own appeal. Public sympathy for Berkman and the San Francisco defendants was growing, so Goldman was not harassed too often by police—except in New York. She responded to the threats of the U.S. marshal there by appearing onstage gagged with a handkerchief.

Despite her successes while awaiting the appeal of her case, Goldman suspected she would ultimately return to jail. The 1917 Espionage Act had outlawed public remarks directed against "the operation of the armed forces." In 1918 the act was amended, establishing a penalty of up to 20 years in prison for anyone who would "utter, print, write, or publish any disloyal, profane, scurrilous, or abusive language about the form of government of the United States, or the Constitution of the United States, or the uniform of the Army and Navy of the United States." This legislation opened the way for a wholesale crackdown on radical activity during World War I and the years that followed.

Mother Earth was among the first casualties of the restrictive laws. The postmaster general declared it "unmailable" in August 1917, blocking its distribution. Undeterred, Goldman, Reitman, Eleanor Fitzgerald, and Stella Comminsky Ballantine started an eight-page *Mother Earth Bulletin* in October. The first issue's headline shouted FREEDOM OF CRITICISM AND OPINION FORBIDDEN, but the bulletin too came under the postal ban six months later.

Few expressed surprise when the Supreme Court declared the Selective Service Act constitutional and upheld the convictions of those prosecuted under its provisions. Goldman and Berkman devoted their remaining weeks of freedom to the organization of the Political Prisoners' Amnesty League to assist jailed dissenters. In February 1918, Goldman arrived at the federal penitentiary in Jefferson City, Missouri.

A flier advertises Goldman and Berkman as speakers at a No-Conscription League rally. The rebels' antidraft efforts led to their imprisonment and exile from the United States.

77

This photograph of Goldman was taken just before she entered the federal penitentiary in 1918. She found conditions there tolerable but noted that "life in prison, unless one has vital interests outside, is deadly dull."

"Greater heroes and martyrs than I have paid for their ideals with prison and death," Goldman wrote to Stella Comminsky Ballantine, "so why not I?" In prison she was assigned to the sewing shop, where each worker had an extremely demanding task to perform each day. Those who failed to satisfy the overseers faced severe punishment such as confinement in a dirty, dark "blind" cell. Now 48, Goldman suffered back and neck pain from straining

to sew her daily quota of 54 jackets. Other prisoners, more practiced at the work, often helped her.

In return, Goldman spoke up for her fellow prisoners and shared the food sent by her comrades. The generous radical easily won the devotion of her fellow inmates. Kate Richards O'Hare, a socialist antiwar protester who entered Jefferson City a year after Goldman, wrote admiringly that the anarchist "mothered and babied . . . every creature in the prison." O'Hare and Goldman became confidantes, initiating a friendly rivalry to see who could do the most to improve prison conditions. Camaraderie such as this, plus continuing support from outside prison and Goldman's undying belief in her ideal, combined to help her survive the ordeal of incarceration.

But while in jail, Goldman felt frustrated that she could do nothing about events taking place outside the penitentiary's walls. The new espionage and sedition laws had given federal and state governments powerful weapons in the war on dissent: 1918 marked the start of what one historian has called "the Great Repression." Goldman's mail was read and censored; the federal government kept files on 8,000 former subscribers to *Mother Earth*. J. Edgar Hoover, an ambitious young official in the Bureau of Investigation (later known as the FBI), started keeping his famous index of alleged radicals and subversives. One police official noted that Goldman was in fact fortunate to be arrested early, under the draft act. Those tried later, such as Socialist

While Goldman awaited deportation with Berkman, a reporter asked her, "That is the end . . . isn't it?" Goldman shot back, "It may only be the beginning."

The USS Buford, *which Goldman referred to as a "battered old tub," transported 249 American exiles to the Soviet Union. The trip took 28 days.*

party leader and presidential candidate Eugene Debs, received much harsher sentences as the Red Scare spread.

The end of World War I in November 1918 did little to calm the antiradical hysteria sweeping the country. Anxious Americans were dismayed by events in Russia, where the October Revolution of 1917 had brought the communist Bolsheviks to power. A postwar economic slump at home, coupled with workers' unwillingness to give up the jobs that wartime necessity had gained for them, helped make 1919 a record year for strikes. The particularly difficult position of minority laborers sparked a number of race riots as well. Radicals were still equated with

foreigners, to the injury of both. U.S. attorney general A. Mitchell Palmer gladly gave in to popular pressure and began a program of deportation.

Under a 1918 antianarchist immigration law, any noncitizen could be ordered to leave the country for the crime of belonging to a subversive organization. Emma Goldman and Alexander Berkman were among the first targets of this statute. The federal government initiated hearings in anticipation of their release from prison. Convinced that he had no hope under the new law, Berkman refused to answer questions. Goldman, however, defended her citizenship on the grounds that her deceased former husband, Jacob Kershner, had been illegally denaturalized a decade earlier. Called before the immigration board one month after her release in September 1919, she vigorously argued that no tribunal had the right to pass judgment on her opinions. She also denounced official efforts to "stifle the voice of the people" and the hopes of labor, but the board ignored her and ruled that she should be deported.

"I consider it an honor," Goldman later said, "to be the first political agitator to be deported from the United States." Determined to the end, she left on a cross-country speaking tour with Berkman. Thousands came to hear the famous rebels lecture on the promise of the Russian Revolution and the tragedy of American repression.

Soon the government closed the case and ordered Goldman and Berkman to Ellis Island to await deportation. The wait turned out to be several weeks long, so Goldman used the time to secure supplies for the ocean voyage and enjoy final visits with devoted family and friends. "It is bitter hard to go," she wrote to Ben Reitman. "But I am proud. . . . No matter where I am, my work for the American Revolution can go on."

Early in the morning of December 21, 1919, Emma Goldman, Alexander Berkman, and 247 other deportees were herded onto the USS *Buford*—the "Red Ark"—a ship bound for Russia. As the old boat steamed quietly out of New York harbor, it passed the Statue of Liberty, which stood staring into the darkness.

Goldman arrived in the Soviet Union eager to discover what the workers' revolution of 1917 had wrought. Her high hopes, however, were soon dashed.

SEVEN

Woman Without a Country

Goldman described her four weeks aboard the USS *Buford* as nothing less than "ghastly." She shared a cabin with the two other female deportees while the 246 male prisoners, guarded by an equal number of soldiers, crowded into the damp hold. As the acknowledged leader of the prisoners, Berkman bargained with the captain of the leaky ship for better food and less oppressive rules. The ample supplies brought by the *Buford*'s two most famous passengers also helped ameliorate the abysmal conditions.

During the voyage, Goldman had time to reflect on the life she was leaving behind and to wonder about the future that awaited her in Russia. Her letters to Stella Comminsky Ballantine reveal both sadness at leaving the United States and excitement at the prospect of life in *matushka Rossiya*—

mother Russia. Not only was Russia Goldman's birthplace, it was, in her mind, a land of revolutionary heroes. There, nearly three years earlier, the tyrannical czar had been deposed and a parliament had been established. A few months later, Russian workers, peasants, and even soldiers had risen up against that new government, allowing the Bolsheviks (orthodox communists led by Vladimir Ilyich Lenin, Leon Trotsky, Grigory Zinovyev, and others) to seize power in what came to be known as the October Revolution of 1917. Like most radicals in North America and Europe, Goldman had cheered the creation of a workers' republic and celebrated the Bolshevik goal of a worldwide working-class revolution.

Received in the Soviet Union as distinguished comrades, Goldman and

Soviet experts examine the crown jewels of the Russian royal family. To her dismay, Goldman found that the new government had not distributed the country's wealth among the masses.

Berkman were immediately taken to the capital city, Petrograd (now Leningrad), to meet important Bolshevik leaders. Only later did they discover that their fellow exiles were detained for days and lectured on the necessity of obedience to the state. But Goldman and Berkman soon had their own lessons in the realities of the "new Russia." Continuing civil unrest and an invasion by the Soviet Union's former allies—capitalist countries such as the United States and Great Britain—had given Lenin an excuse to take complete control, through the Central Committee, of all aspects of Russian life.

Lenin stripped local *soviets* (workers' councils) throughout the countryside of their power, centralizing the government and making it easier to direct. The Central Committee ignored the revolutionary principle of classlessness and established 34 grades of supply rations for workers in different occupations. *Propusks* (permits of identification) made free movement between cities impossible for most citizens, and strict curfews were established. Goldman described Moscow as an "armed camp" where the Cheka (secret police) terrorized everyone on the pretense of rooting out traitors. Forced collectivization of all resources seemed not to work at all: Cityfolk and countryfolk alike starved by the millions. The government, meanwhile, blamed all of the country's problems on the allied capitalist nations and the evil forces of counterrevolution.

But perhaps the most bitter pill for Goldman to swallow was the violent suppression of dissent. Free speech was stifled everywhere, even at Communist party meetings. Native Russian anarchists told Goldman of raids on their headquarters, censorship and confiscation of their papers, jailings, and executions. A very troubled Goldman sought out the comrades she most respected, hoping they could help her understand the situation. Longtime friend John Reed, whose *Ten Days That Shook the World* chronicled the historic events of October 1917, argued that the actions were necessary to guarantee the success of the Revolution. Maxim Gorky,

Russian peasants discuss communism. Although the common people had given the revolution its momentum, they did not at first benefit from the Bolshevik victory.

Goldman was shocked by the murderous activities of the Soviet Cheka, or secret police, which sought to suppress dissent. Here, some of its victims lie in a Petrograd street.

the renowned Russian playwright and a Communist party official, agreed. Neither man, however, could convince Goldman that such oppressive measures would advance the cause of the workers.

A sympathetic veteran of the revolutionary movement arranged a meeting between Goldman, Berkman, and Lenin, the mastermind of Bolshevik Russia. The American anarchists presented a petition from their beleaguered Russian comrades, only to hear the Communist party chief dismiss their plea for freedom of speech as mere "sentimentality." Urging the duo to find productive work for the revolution, Lenin simultaneously placed restrictions on

their activities. When Goldman and Berkman proposed the establishment of Russian Friends of American Freedom, an organization designed to promote a workers' revolution in the United States, Lenin required that it be placed securely under Bolshevik authority. The rebels decided against working within the confines of the bureaucracy.

The exiles did their best to become useful comrades, but their efforts to contribute—Goldman in a hospital, Berkman in soup kitchens—met with profound indifference from officials. Finally, an opportunity arose that seemed to allow for individual initiative: They received an offer to travel with a small group of scholars collecting testimony and documents for the Petrograd Museum of the Revolution. In an ancient, specially outfitted Pullman railway car, the group left for the Ukraine region at the end of June 1920.

For eight months the museum staff hitched its car to trains all over Russia. Everywhere they heard tales of suffering endured both before and after the events of October 1917. Goldman and Berkman received a warm welcome from the people, especially once they explained that they were foreign comrades with neither the power nor the desire to confiscate goods in the name of the Revolution. Goldman despaired as she observed the continuing "silent pogrom" directed against Russia's Jewish communities. And everywhere, the violent repression of non-Bolshevik activists went on.

Invited to join the underground anarchist movement, Goldman declined; she did not want to work against the new Soviet state while it remained under attack from the outside world. But she felt ambivalent about the Russian Revolution, which did not resemble any revolution she or her fellow American radicals had envisioned. For the first time in modern history, the world had witnessed a popular revolt that in the end only imposed more severe limits on a people's freedom. And the strayed uprising had been based on ideals Goldman had spent a lifetime defending. "My old values had been shipwrecked and I myself thrown overboard to sink or swim," she wrote of her disappointment in Russia. Gold-

While traveling through the Soviet countryside in 1920 and 1921, Goldman snapped this picture of a young famine victim. Bolshevik incompetence resulted in widespread suffering.

man grew increasingly disconcerted as Berkman clung to hope that the Bolsheviks would eventually prove their commitment to the workers and abolish "war communism." The old friends argued endlessly about the theory and reality of revolution.

Goldman's sense of loss deepened with the deaths of her sister Helena in America, her radical comrade John Reed, and Peter Kropotkin, the sage of the anarchist movement, who died just days after she visited his bedside. Gold-

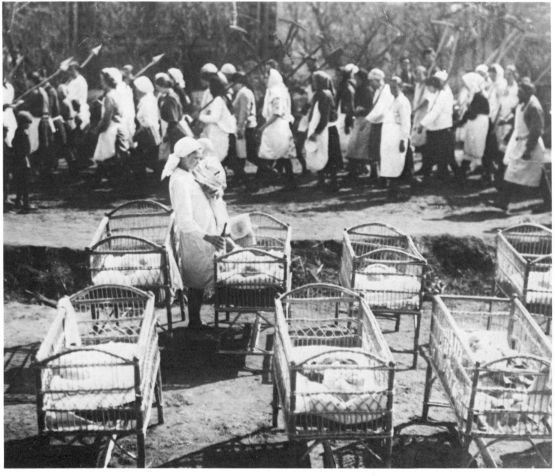

A Soviet day-care worker attends to her charges while women head for a day of work in the fields. Goldman only rarely saw such evidence of the revolution's success.

man and Berkman resigned their posts with the Museum of the Revolution and set to work on a Kropotkin Memorial Museum. More and more, it seemed that the Bolsheviks could stomach anarchists only in museums—or prisons. The two exiles could no longer accept the Soviet government's authoritarianism.

Goldman and Berkman made their final break with the Soviet Union when workers in several Petrograd factories struck for better rations. Denunciations of the workers by Bolshevik leaders spurred a sympathy strike by the sailors of Kronstadt. The mariners were loyal anarchists who also circulated demands for freedom of speech and assembly. In March 1921, Leon Trotsky, head of the Red Army, pronounced Kronstadt in rebellion and bombarded the city, killing hundreds and wounding thousands. Goldman and Berkman could do nothing. They too were suspected of disloyalty to the Revolution and risked official retribution if they dared speak out against the massacre. The evidence was now overwhelming: Bolshevik policy was to betray the workers whenever the Revolution—as defined by the Bolsheviks—was threatened.

Severing all ties to the Soviet government, Goldman and Berkman supported themselves with money sent by American friends. Their home became a haven for persecuted anarchists and newly arrived American expatriates. The two activists worked to free dissidents from Soviet jails but found officials unwilling to help those deemed uncooperative individualists. They resolved to leave the Soviet Union for good. When an invitation to the Berlin Anarchist Congress provided a reason to travel, Goldman and Berkman successfully applied for passports. The Bolsheviks allowed them to leave but made their displeasure clearly known.

Goldman and Berkman were detained in the western Soviet province of Latvia and denied entrance to Germany. Physically and emotionally drained, they accepted temporary refuge in the Swedish port of Stockholm. The Swedish government discouraged the newcomers from speaking or writing about political repression in the USSR and in the end asked them to

Goldman speaks at the 1921 funeral of Peter Kropotkin while Berkman (seated, left) looks on. She mourned Kropotkin's death as the "loss of a great moral force."

leave Sweden permanently. Radical colleagues throughout Europe petitioned their governments to grant asylum to the exiles. Finally, Berkman smuggled himself into Germany; Goldman soon followed on a temporary visa.

Driven by her convictions to protest the Bolshevik abandonment of the Revolution, Goldman wrote several articles intended for publication in radical American magazines. But the journals still supported the Soviet Union and refused to print her attacks. Goldman would not accept the hateful alternative of selling her articles to anticommunist periodicals that would all too gladly print criticisms of the Bolsheviks. She finally sold a series of essays to the *New York World*, and soon her unflattering portrayal of the Soviet state elicited furious denunciations from American Communists. The money brought in by the article, however, allowed Goldman to rent an apartment in Berlin and settle temporarily among the growing émigré community there.

Goldman devoted much of 1922 to writing a book about her Russian experience. In it, she hoped to discredit Bolshevism and defend her revolutionary ideals. True communism never existed in the Soviet Union, she claimed, since the class system—the division of society into different levels of privilege and wealth—was only reshaped, not abolished. Further, the Bolsheviks wielded even more power than had their predecessors, the czars, and party officers spent most of their time jockeying for greater influence and prestige. In Goldman's view, only "an emphatic veto upon all tyranny and centralization" and a genuine revision of "economic, social, and cultural values . . . [could] secure the Revolution."

Goldman sold the manuscript, entitled "My Two Years in Russia," but found the buyer slow to produce a book. After months of delay the text was sold to a second publisher, which finally brought it out in 1923 under the title *My Disillusionment in Russia*. But the last twelve chapters had been accidentally left out. Devastated, Goldman insisted on the publication of the deleted material. A second book, *My Further Disillusionment in Russia*, ap-

peared in 1924, but in the long run the bungled project gained little popular attention.

Goldman's two years in Berlin did hold some joy. She and Berkman received many visitors, including her niece Stella Comminsky Ballantine. Yet the limitations of exile irritated her. Accustomed to constant work and public attention, Goldman chafed under German restrictions on her activity. On pain of expulsion, she was forbidden to agitate against political repression in the Soviet Union. Unable to speak or profitably publish the articles she wrote, Goldman accepted the suggestion of friends and looked to England for a new beginning.

But in the wake of World War I the British had cracked down on dissent. When she arrived in England in the summer of 1924, Goldman discovered that the anarchist movement there had been stamped out by deportations and internal divisions. Deprived of political comradeship, she made connections in London's intellectual community, including a rewarding friendship with influential critic and novelist Rebecca West. West later described Goldman as "one of the great people of the world . . . a mountain of integrity. I do not know how one would set about destroying Emma, except by frequent charges of high explosive."

The writer agreed to help organize a dinner that would both introduce Goldman to British literary society and launch a campaign for the release of Russian political prisoners. Goldman's debut, however, was less than successful. Applause turned to stunned silence and then angry protest as the guest of honor decried Bolshevik tyranny. Socialists in the audience condemned Goldman, claiming she had betrayed her own radical past.

Disappointed with her reception among the intelligentsia, Goldman resolved to return to the public platform. West and other friends warned her that lecture work did not pay in England unless speakers had famous supporters and did intense advance work. Goldman sent appeals to potential sponsors; their replies filled her social calendar with teas and parties but provided few financial backers. Most, such as Bertrand Russell, the great mathematician and philosopher who had himself visited Russia, thought it bad politics to attack the world's first workers' state. In her own words, Goldman was "proscribed by both sides, the communist and the capitalist." She tramped twice each week from one end of London to another, exhorting disappointingly small audiences to support the political victims of the Russian dictatorship.

Goldman then took a brief tour of Wales, where she met an old associate named James Colton. Aware of her precarious alien status, he proposed marriage. In order to avoid deportation from Great Britain, Goldman accepted Colton's offer and gained British citizenship. Citizenship, however, meant only one kind of security. Goldman continued to depend financially on family and friends. Hoping to earn her own keep, she launched a series of lectures on drama. She enjoyed a sum-

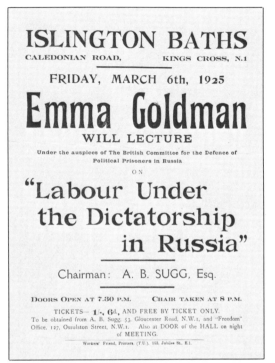

ISLINGTON BATHS
CALEDONIAN ROAD,   KINGS CROSS, N.1

FRIDAY, MARCH 6th, 1925

Emma Goldman
WILL LECTURE

Under the auspices of The British Committee for the Defence of Political Prisoners in Russia
ON

"Labour Under the Dictatorship in Russia"

Chairman: A. B. SUGG, Esq.

DOORS OPEN AT 7.30 P.M.   CHAIR TAKEN AT 8 P.M.
TICKETS— 1/-, 6d, AND FREE BY TICKET ONLY.
To be obtained from A. B. Sugg, 53, Gloucester Road, N.W.1, and "Freedom" Office, 127, Ossulston Street, N.W.1.   Also at DOOR of the HALL on night of MEETING.
Workers' Friend, Printers, (T.U.), 163, Jubilee St., E.1.

In England, Goldman married to obtain citizenship and attempted to launch a speaking career. But audience response was lukewarm, and her efforts proved unprofitable.

mer of research in the British Museum, then traveled to many cities to speak on the work of a wide range of playwrights. Audiences enjoyed Goldman's speeches, but the effort did not earn enough to pay the costs of travel and hall rental.

Goldman's final disappointment in England came during the 1926 general strike in London. She offered to help the unions but was turned down by labor leaders who feared her radical reputation. Disgusted, she departed for St. Tropez, France, where friends had

Barred from the United States, Goldman could do nothing to help anarchists Bartolomeo Vanzetti (center left) and Nicola Sacco (center right), who were executed in 1927.

bought her a small cottage with a garden. There she set to work on a book to be entitled "Foremost Russian Dramatists."

The frustrations that Goldman encountered in her work paralleled a deep sense of personal loneliness. As she wrote to Berkman, she was "consumed by longing for love and affection for some human being of my own." Occasional visitors and frequent correspondence with friends only heightened Goldman's desire for close companionship. Loneliness, she believed, was the price a woman paid for living on the cusp of change. "We [women] are removed only by a very short period from our traditions, the tradition of being loved, cared for, secured," she wrote. "The modern woman cannot be the wife and mother in the old sense, and the new medium has not yet been devised, I mean the way of being wife, mother, friend, and yet retain[ing] one's own complete freedom. Will it ever?"

But at 57, Goldman was not ready to accept loneliness as her lot in life. In the autumn of 1926 she embarked upon an expedition to Canada. Soon after arriving in Montreal she started a secret love affair with Leon Malmed, a married comrade from Albany, New York. With renewed energy, she survived lukewarm receptions from audiences in Montreal and Winnipeg to galvanize the cities of Edmonton and Toronto. She remained in Toronto for most of 1927, successfully lecturing on literature, birth control, and political freedom.

Emotional reunions with family members reminded Goldman of the proximity of the forbidden United States. She desperately wished to return to live in her adopted country, but the deportation order would never be reversed, despite her admirers' efforts. In exile, Goldman despaired that she could do nothing to help Nicola Sacco and Bartolomeo Vanzetti, immigrant Boston anarchists executed in 1927 after the most controversial murder trial of the decade. Addressing halls that were sometimes full and sometimes empty taxed her almost beyond endurance. Her troubles and worries were all the more difficult to bear because she bore them alone. "Somehow it was easier when I could make the struggle

In 1927, Goldman settled into Bon Esprit, a cottage in St. Tropez, France, to write her autobiography. She would live there for most of the rest of her life.

with you," she wrote to Berkman, who was residing in France, "but now, alone, it is hard. . . ."

Inspired by visitors such as Ben Reitman, who brought her hundreds of the letters she had written over the years as well as his own set of *Mother Earth* magazines, Goldman's thoughts turned to the past. She began to consider working on the autobiography she had often been urged to write. Early in 1928, with money she had saved in Canada and $2,500 raised by supporters in New York, Goldman sailed for France. Awaiting her there was her St. Tropez cottage and the task of reliving her life.

The rise of fascism in Europe worried Goldman during her final years, but the struggle against fascists in Spain gave her a glimpse of the revolution she had always dreamed of.

EIGHT

A Voice in the Wilderness

The agonizing process of writing her autobiography, entitled *Living My Life*, took Goldman two full years. Throughout the process Berkman lent his invaluable editorial skills and steadfast companionship, as did a young writer, Emily Coleman, who served as Goldman's secretary. When completed, Goldman's vivid, moving life story filled two volumes and garnered wide praise for its honesty and clarity. Regrettably for the author, sales in the United States of *Living My Life* did not keep pace with its critical success, since few in the Great Depression year of 1931 could afford the publisher's price tag of $7.50.

The publication of her memoirs did not lift the dejection that had plagued Goldman since her deportation from the United States. In America, she had often had to choose between public and private fulfillment; now, she was both lonely and inactive. Friends who visited St. Tropez for even a few days found their depressed host difficult and unpleasant company. Her strong personality, Berkman noted, had "a squelching effect" on others that the frustrations of exile only aggravated. Berkman's own relationship with Goldman became strained after jealous exchanges between Goldman and Emmy Eckstein, Berkman's companion.

Goldman sought to fend off her misery by returning to active work. But in Europe her radical ideas were usually dismissed—as they had been in America—as hopelessly visionary and thus unimportant. "We are voices in the wilderness," she wrote Berkman, "voices for liberty. No one wants it anymore." Indeed, freedom in nations

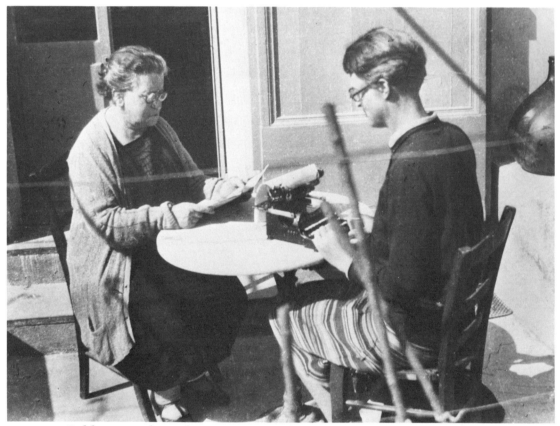

Goldman works on her memoirs with an aide. Some critics called the book "a thousand dull pages of fornication and fanaticism," but most praised its "frank, direct, and brisk" style.

around the globe was now threatened by a powerful new menace, the fascism of Germany's Adolf Hitler and Italy's Benito Mussolini. The fascists endorsed a philosophy of fanatical nationalism and strict government control over all aspects of life. Many of its opponents had embraced the dreary Soviet-style communism that Goldman had found so oppressive. The anarchist often felt as if she had outlived her dream of personal freedom for all.

Over the next few years Goldman's life followed a regular pattern: When she was active, she felt invigorated and defiant; when she was prevented from speaking out, she brooded and despaired. During periods of inactivity, her efforts to keep busy in the kitchen and garden of her cottage, Bon Esprit, did little to lift her mood. A spring 1932 lecture tour took her to Scandinavia and Germany, where she promoted her book and discussed the evils of dictatorship. The next year, however, Hitler's rise to power prevented a return trip. Goldman traveled instead to England, where her early warnings of the fascist threat were received with skepticism. Holland allowed the veteran rebel to make only three speeches before supplying her with a stern warning and a one-way ticket out of the country. "You are still dangerous—there is no doubt of it," Berkman wrote her approvingly.

Thwarted in Europe, Goldman looked westward for an audience. Influential friends, among them some of the best-known writers and intellectuals in America, lobbied the United States government for a reprieve for Goldman. They were optimistic about their chances because the country's mood had changed since Goldman's deportation. President Franklin D. Roosevelt's more liberal administration and the sympathy of Secretary of Labor Frances Perkins, the first woman cabinet member, made at least a temporary stay appear possible. Anticipating success, Goldman traveled to Canada in December 1933. She soon learned that a three-month visa had been granted. After 14 years of wandering, the 64-year-old exile would return home.

At first, Goldman balked at the government's requirement that she limit her speeches to the subjects of drama and literature. But American Civil Liberties Union president Roger Baldwin assured her that she could take her old approach to those topics, using them to address any number of social problems. An excited Goldman came south by

An unrelenting champion of individual freedom, Goldman deplored the rise of fascist leaders such as Italy's Benito Mussolini (left) and Germany's Adolf Hitler (right).

train and arrived in New York's Grand Central Station alone, as she had 45 years before. The press conferences and interviews began as soon as she arrived at her hotel. Except for attacks by the communist press, Goldman thought the media coverage of her visit fairer than any she had ever received. After an emotional dinner of welcome and a lecture at Town Hall, she departed for a speaking tour.

Unfortunately, the 1934 tour seemed to Goldman both a personal and finan-

Goldman speaks with reporters upon arriving in the United States for her 1934 visit. She treasured the three months she was allowed to spend with old friends and new admirers.

cial failure. She later described "city after city, with huge halls, and only a handful of people present." The disappointing turnouts were partly the result of a boycott sponsored by American Communists, who despised Goldman for her stand on the Soviet Union. But the real problem was bad planning. The entrepreneur to whom Goldman had entrusted the arrangements repeatedly miscalculated, renting enormous auditoriums and charging prohibitive admission fees. One of Goldman's few

triumphs came in Chicago, where Ben Reitman and other old comrades handled her publicity: Several thousand listeners attended each of her lectures there. In May 1934, Goldman crossed the border back to Canada. There, she conducted regular anarchist meetings in Montreal and Toronto and wrote essays commissioned by American magazines.

Despite its setbacks, Goldman's trip to America had reminded her of the joys of an active life. To Berkman, who remained skeptical, she wrote of a freshness in the American air, an openness to change she thought absent in other lands: "I felt twenty years off my shoulders because everywhere I met wide awake people who were really intensely interested in ideas." Among those "wide awake people" was a 36-year-old doctor and graduate student named Frank Heiner. Goldman had immediately been drawn to this intelligent, handsome admirer who had accomplished much despite being blind since childhood. With the knowledge and grudging acceptance of Heiner's wife, who typed and read letters aloud for her husband, the pair exchanged love notes for several months. Although flattered by his attention, Goldman at first refused Heiner's requests to come visit her in Canada. But finally her loneliness overcame her caution, and Heiner came to Toronto for a two-week stay. Goldman reveled in her renewed happiness, only to feel the pain of separation for months after Heiner returned to America. When it became clear that the United States would not grant her a second visa, an exhausted Goldman left for France.

Goldman's loneliness weighed on her all the more heavily after her return to Europe. The company of Berkman and Eckstein failed to soothe her wounds, and within a few months the couple departed for nearby Nice. Restless, Goldman planned another trip. The British finally appeared interested in her stinging comparison of Bolshevism and fascism. She threw herself into a round of speaking and social

Alexander Berkman, Goldman's closest friend and ally, took his own life in 1936, writing that "it is time to clear out." The loss of her comrade of 47 years crushed Goldman.

engagements in London and a lecture tour of Wales. But while Goldman toured Great Britain, Berkman's health deteriorated. Two operations failed to rid him of his newly detected cancer, so Goldman returned to France to be near her closest friend. On June 27, 1936 (Goldman's 67th birthday), Berkman, nearly paralyzed by pain, fatally shot himself. Desolate, Goldman wrote a memorial letter to comrades, helped

*Spanish radicals parade through the streets of Madrid during the
Spanish civil war. Goldman called the Spanish revolutionaries a
"shining example to the rest of the world."*

make financial arrangements for Eckstein, and searched for a way to carry on the struggle.

World events soon presented Goldman with the opportunity she had been hoping for. The international anarchist movement had found a compelling new cause when a series of unanticipated changes electrified Spain. In 1931 a genuinely democratic republic had emerged there, giving those who did not own land a real voice in government for the first time. Over the next five years the left-wing Popular Front (which included democrats, socialists, communists, and anarchists—those who favored more popular involvement in government) had struggled with the right-wing Nationalists (which promised the country "religion, law, and order") for control. When the Popular Front narrowly won the 1936 elections, segments of the Spanish army launched a revolt under the leadership of General Francisco Franco. The nation split into a Nationalist and a republican zone, and a bloody civil war commenced.

Catalonia and Aragon, the strongly anarchist provinces of the republican zone, soon seemed to embody the revolution long envisioned by Goldman and her comrades. Farms, factories, and the militia underwent local collectivization: Peasants and workers simply took over production for the shared benefit of all. A few months after the start of the civil war, proanarchist political organizations such as the Free Women (Mujos Libres), the National Confederation of Labor (CNT), and the Anarchist Federation of Iberia (FAI)

wrote to Goldman asking for help. They invited her to visit Spain and lend her voice to the libertarian struggle.

Ecstatic, Goldman immediately accepted the invitation. Within weeks, she arrived in Barcelona. There she was thrilled to receive a regal welcome in a truly anarchist city. Still more gratifying was her tour through Catalonia and Aragon, where the anarchist ideal of local autonomy and voluntary cooperation between communities seemed to have come to life. "Never again will anyone dare to say that Anarchism is not practical or that we have no program," she wrote triumphantly. "It is my grandest hour."

The matriarch of the revolution offered her services as a nurse or cook, but CNT-FAI organizers insisted she would be most effective if she broadcasted the news of Spain's achievements to the English-speaking world. Goldman reluctantly returned to London to write and speak about the Spanish civil war and to edit an English-language version of the CNT-FAI bulletin. In fund-raising speeches she simultaneously celebrated the anarchists' victories in Spain, defended their participation in the Popular Front coalition, and warned of the threat posed by the fascists supported by Hitler and Mussolini. But the fascists were not the only force that cast the outcome of the civil war into doubt.

The CNT-FAI was only one part of a diverse Popular Front. The anarchists soon found themselves compromising with less radical elements of the republican-zone government. Some even ac-

Goldman meets with CNT-FAI comrades in Spain. Although she privately disagreed with some of the group's policies, Goldman was a staunch public supporter of its goals.

cepted posts in the new cabinet, an unheard-of move for anarchists, who did not believe in institutionalized government. As an official representative of the CNT-FAI, Goldman publicly supported its actions, but as an unyielding idealist she privately criticized the leadership's decisions. The inconsistency between the anarchist vision and the political reality troubled her deeply.

The prospects for anarchism in Spain dimmed as other democratic nations adopted a policy of neutrality. The Spanish republicans thus received vitally needed aid only from the Stalinist Soviet Union. Communists soon dominated the antifascist effort and persecuted the non-Communists within the

Popular Front—especially the anarchists. During the May Days of 1937, anarchist workers battled Communist-led police in Barcelona for control of the cooperatively run telephone headquarters; anarchist leaders lost still more power as a result of the clash. And while internal strife weakened the republicans, generous support from Germany and Italy bolstered the fascist Nationalists. The worsening situation distressed Goldman. Only when she returned to Catalonia to witness the continuing creative efforts of the common people did she feel reassured. She continued to work for the tragically handicapped CNT-FAI leadership.

Barcelona fell to the fascists in January 1939; by April, Franco's Nationalist forces controlled the entire nation. Goldman soon launched a campaign to aid the thousands of anarchist refugees who fled Spain fearing for their lives. After encountering apathy in England, she sailed the Atlantic Ocean for the last time, hoping to rouse Canadian and American consciences on behalf of the Spanish homeless.

But Goldman herself was a refugee with persistent financial woes of her own. Funds from the sale of Bon Esprit in 1937 barely paid Emmy Eckstein's hospital bills, fulfilling a promise Goldman had made to Berkman. Lecturing provided little surplus income, so Goldman still depended on gifts from friends. The warm tributes she received on her 70th birthday did little to counteract her returning depression. Shortly thereafter, in the autumn of 1939, Goldman was warned by the Canadian government not to speak out on certain topics. Although she wanted to protest the approach of another world war, she feared that arrest would mean deportation to England. Then the United States offered her another visa on the condition that she testify before the Dies committee, a congressional body investigating alleged subversive activity. Goldman chose to remain true to her revolutionist ethics. Her exile continued.

The aging Goldman was saved from outright despair by one final cause. In Canada, her anarchist associates were experiencing increased harassment at the hands of the government. Arturo Bortolotti, one of four Italian anarchists arrested for "possession of subversive

With the aid of Italy and Germany, Spanish general Francisco Franco led fascist forces to victory in 1939. He ruled Spain until his death in 1975.

literature," faced deportation to fascist Italy, which meant certain death. Goldman embarked on a rigorous letter-writing and fund-raising campaign on behalf of the jailed Italian. Content in her work, she pursued Bortolotti's cause into the winter months despite doctors' pleas that she rest. When he

By the time she died on May 14, 1940, 70-year-old Emma Goldman had, in her own words, "drunk the cup to the last drop."

was released on bail, Bortolotti became Goldman's constant companion, often taking her from Toronto to the Canadian-American border, where she would tearfully stare at her forbidden homeland.

In February 1940, while working on Bortolotti's case, Goldman suffered a massive stroke. Unable to talk or move her right side, she remained bedridden for three months, surviving just long enough to learn of Bortolotti's victory in his fight against deportation. Emma Goldman finally let go of life on May 14, 1940. Canadian authorities returned her body to the United States, where grieving friends and followers mourned her death. "Emma came back today in a baggage car," Ben Reitman wrote bitterly to a friend. "She gave 50 years of her precious life trying to make America a better place to live in and to stop war. And the only way she could get back to America was in a steel casket."

Goldman was interred at Waldheim Cemetery in Chicago, yards from the monument to the Haymarket martyrs, whose death had inspired her to a life of activism. The inscription on that monument reads: "The day will come when our silence will be more powerful than the voices you are throttling today."

Like the Haymarket martyrs, Emma Goldman left a legacy of fierce commitment to the ideals of freedom and equality. In the United States, protection of civil liberties still waxes and wanes with the political climate, but the tradition bequeathed by Goldman and other radicals makes it less likely that the majority will ever silence any unpopular minority. Workers, women, and minorities still suffer oppression and discrimination, but they suffer a little less because idealists like Goldman shed light on the abuse of power. In her later years, Goldman longed to return to America precisely because she saw its great capacity for change and growth. Today, she might take pride in what the hundred years since her arrival have wrought. More likely, Emma Goldman would scold us for complacency, for looking back, instead of forward, to the struggle for freedom.

FURTHER READING

Drinnon, Richard. *Rebel in Paradise: A Biography of Emma Goldman.* Chicago: University of Chicago Press, 1961.

————, and Anna Marie Drinnon, eds. *Nowhere at Home: Letters from Exile of Emma Goldman and Alexander Berkman.* New York: Schocken, 1975.

Falk, Candace. *Love, Anarchy, and Emma Goldman.* New York: Holt, Rinehart & Winston, 1984.

Goldman, Emma. *Anarchism and Other Essays.* New York: Dover, 1969.

————. *Living My Life.* 2 vols. New York: Dover, 1970.

————. *My Disillusionment in Russia.* New York: Doubleday, Page, 1923.

————. *My Further Disillusionment in Russia.* New York: Doubleday, Page, 1924.

————. *The Social Significance of Modern Drama.* New York: Applause Theatre Books, 1987.

Marsh, Margaret. *Anarchist Women, 1870–1920.* Philadelphia: Temple University Press, 1981.

Porter, David, ed. *Vision on Fire: Emma Goldman on the Spanish Revolution.* New York: Commonground Press, 1983.

Shulman, Alix Kates, ed. *Red Emma Speaks: Selected Writings and Speeches of Emma Goldman.* New York: Random House, 1972.

Solomon, Martha. *Emma Goldman.* Boston: Twayne, 1987.

Wexler, Alice. *Emma Goldman in America.* Boston: Beacon Press, 1984.

————. *Emma Goldman in Exile.* Boston: Beacon Press, 1989.

CHRONOLOGY

June 27, 1869	Emma Goldman born in Kovno, Lithuania, a province of the Russian Empire
1885	Immigrates to the United States; settles in Rochester, New York
1886	Marries Jacob Kershner, becoming a U.S. citizen
1887	Four anarchists are hanged in Chicago after a riot in Haymarket Square; the event radicalizes Goldman
1889	Goldman divorces Kershner and moves to New York City; meets Alexander Berkman
1890	Conducts her first speaking tour
1892	Berkman attempts to assassinate industrialist Henry Clay Frick and is sentenced to 22 years in prison; Goldman is suspected of complicity
1893	Goldman meets Edward Brady; goes to prison for her role in a labor protest
1895–96	Studies nursing in Europe
1900	Works with the anarchist movement in Europe
1901	Leon Czolgosz assassinates U.S. president William McKinley; police accuse Goldman of conspiracy but cannot prove their charges
1906	Goldman publishes the first issue of *Mother Earth*; Alexander Berkman is released from prison
1908	Goldman meets Dr. Ben L. Reitman
1909	Immigration officials revoke the citizenship of Goldman's ex-husband, rendering her a resident alien
1910	Goldman publishes *Anarchism and Other Essays*
1914	Publishes *The Social Significance of Modern Drama*; launches a campaign for birth control rights
1917	The United States enters World War I; Goldman leads antiwar protests and is convicted of conspiracy to obstruct the draft; the U.S. Postal Service bans *Mother Earth*
1918	Goldman is imprisoned for her antiwar work
1919	The U.S. government deports Goldman and Berkman, sending them to the Soviet Union
1920–21	Goldman travels throughout the Soviet Union
1922	Leaves the Soviet Union for Sweden, then settles in Germany
1923	Publishes *My Disillusionment in Russia*
1924	Moves to England; publishes *My Further Disillusionment in Russia*
1925	Gains British citizenship
1926–27	Conducts a speaking tour of Canada; settles in St. Tropez, France
1931	Publishes her autobiography, *Living My Life*
1934	Spends three months in the United States
1936	Berkman dies; Goldman visits Spain to lend support to anarchist rebels during the civil war
1939	Goldman moves to Canada
1940	Emma Goldman dies at the age of 70

INDEX

PICTURE CREDITS

David Waldstreicher is a graduate of the University of Virginia, where he studied history and English literature. Awarded a Mellon Fellowship in the humanities, he is currently enrolled in the doctoral program in American studies at Yale University. Mr. Waldstreicher is also the author of *The Armenian Americans*, a volume in Chelsea House's THE PEOPLES OF NORTH AMERICA series.

❖   ❖   ❖

Matina S. Horner is president of Radcliffe College and associate professor of psychology and social relations at Harvard University. She is best known for her studies of women's motivation, achievement, and personality development. Dr. Horner serves on several national boards and advisory councils, including those of the National Science Foundation, Time Inc., and the Women's Research and Education Institute. She earned her B.A. from Bryn Mawr College and Ph.D. from the University of Michigan, and holds honorary degrees from many colleges and universities, including Mount Holyoke, Smith, Tufts, and the University of Pennsylvania.